Preparing for Continuous Quality Improvement for Healthcare

Sustainability through Functional Tree Structures

Preparing for Continuous Quality Improvement in Healthcare is a fascinating and yet practical approach to sustainable change for human service systems and institutions. It simply and comprehensively maps out a step by step approach to programmatic and structural change that regular people can understand and apply. Reza Ziaee is a master at his craft and teaches us all that systematic change can be pretty basic.

I wish I had his book in my back pocket when I was the State Director of Michigan's department of Human Services.

Ismael Ahmed
Senior Adviser to the Chancellor and Associate Provost of Metropolitan Impact
University of Michigan Dearborn

The United States Healthcare delivery system is frequently incomprehensible and expensive - just try to find out what the cost of your proposed care will be ahead of time. With a succession of changes in reimbursement methods, healthcare has been in a chaotic transition. The provision of care is not driven by patient centered needs and is highly unfair and fundamentally flawed due in large part to the philosophy that a market based solution can work. Unfortunately, market based solutions have not precipitated a significant improvement in care and have clearly failed to meet the needs of most Americans.

So what is a healthcare leader to do in this chaotic mess? For the last three decades, we have all experienced the costly and impressive "consultants" who have promised programs (process improvement, TQM, CQI, 6-Sigma, Lean, Optimization and many others) but have not produced long term solutions or benefits and worse yet they have not provided a clear path for management to follow.

Reza Ziaee, PhD and James Bologna, in their highly readable and insightful book "*Preparing for Continuous Quality Improvement in Healthcare,*" present a comprehensive approach to understanding and controlling the myriad of processes in a healthcare organization. Ziaee and Bologna analyze our current healthcare situation, identify its many failings and then introduce the concept of Functional Tree Structures, which is a robust tool for process understanding and improvement. This book explains the concepts of stabilizing, optimizing and aligning processes and gives examples how to follow a more structured program that leads to sustainable improvements.

In "*Preparing for Continuous Quality Improvement in Healthcare*" Ziaee and Bologna give us a comprehensive and evidence based method for actually making system wide changes. And if we have the courage to embrace this straightforward method with enlightened leadership, will result in the best healthcare system possible.

Dr. Frank Balestrieri
Anesthesiologist, Banner Medical Group

Performance Improvement is a critical component to the health and well being of healthcare organizations today. As decreased reimbursement pressures continue to deplete operating profits, organizations must find other ways of managing costs rather than the old method of just reducing staff. Many have already reaped the benefits from the "low hanging fruit" initiatives.

The authors of this book have put together an easily read and understandable roadmap to help any organization improve their operating efficiencies. I highly recommend this book and the methods described within.

Mark S. Johnson MA, CPA, FACHE
COO/CFO, Norwood Hospital, Norwood, MA

Preparing for Continuous Quality Improvement in Healthcare, offers an illuminating perspective on building a *sustainable* environment of quality improvement in healthcare. This is not another "project of the day" methodology, but a full model that will leave you with a better health care environment – better outcomes, better care and lower cost.

Deborah Dahl
Vice President, Patient Care Innovation
Banner Health

Reza and James touch on very powerful concepts which allow for the visualization of an organization through Functional Tree Structures (FTS). It provides an elegant contextual understanding of the detailed attributes of an organization and provides leadership with compelling logic for change. FTS also delivers clarity in understanding where improvement will help the organization through a unified understanding of the interrelated functions. FTS provides the platform for lasting change and ongoing viability.

Given the immense complexity inherent in the provision of health services, performance improvement using traditional approaches has not consistently provided consistent ROIs. Many organizations risk demise unless they can manage the task of implementing meaningful, and repeatable, process improvements at a faster pace. I believe that FTS provides a powerful catalyst for performance improvement and ongoing measurement. Following the tools and concepts presented in this book, organizations have greater assurance that goals are met and performance improvement gains are held. Finally, FTS can be used to across the entire organization to assess whether the strategic goals and objectives have been met or sustained.

Shane Wolverton
Senior Vice President
Comparion Medical Analytics

Preparing for Continuous Quality Improvement for Healthcare

Sustainability through Functional Tree Structures

Reza Ziaee,
MA, MSE, MBB, PhD, FHIMSS

James Bologna, MBA

CRC Press
Taylor & Francis Group
Boca Raton   London   New York

CRC Press is an imprint of the
Taylor & Francis Group, an **informa** business

A PRODUCTIVITY PRESS BOOK

CRC Press
Taylor & Francis Group
6000 Broken Sound Parkway NW, Suite 300
Boca Raton, FL 33487-2742

© 2015 by Taylor & Francis Group, LLC
CRC Press is an imprint of Taylor & Francis Group, an Informa business

No claim to original U.S. Government works

Printed on acid-free paper
Version Date: 20140617

International Standard Book Number-13: 978-1-4665-6770-2 (Paperback)

Library of Congress Cataloging-in-Publication Data

Ziaee, Reza, 1949- author.
    Preparing for continuous quality improvement for healthcare : sustainability through functional tree structures / Reza Ziaee and James S. Bologna.
    p. ; cm.
    Includes bibliographical references and index.
    ISBN 978-1-4665-6770-2 (hardcover : alk. paper)
    I. Bologna, James S., 1959- author. II. Title.
    [DNLM: 1. Quality Assurance, Health Care--organization & administration.
2. Delivery of Health Care--organization & administration. 3. Health Services Administration. 4. Organizational Innovation. 5. Quality of Health Care--organization & administration. W 84.41]

    RA971
    362.1068--dc23   2014023176

Visit the Taylor & Francis Web site at
http://www.taylorandfrancis.com

and the CRC Press Web site at
http://www.crcpress.com

Contents

Preface

As firsthand observers of healthcare operations, it appears to us that the challenges healthcare organizations face today build on the challenges we faced 25 years ago. Just as many hospital campuses have grown to become mazes of new construction, the processes that patients and staff work within are equally difficult to navigate. Some of the complications grew from new, complex treatments and technologies, regulations, and competition. Some came with procedures and processes layered on top of existing procedures and policies. Certainly, healthcare has become progressively more sophisticated since the mid-1980s, yet surprisingly, there have not been any consistent, broadly implemented, breakthrough advancements in service, quality, and costs. Quite literally, in many hospitals it appears that we have built on the physical and procedural ruins of past hospital civilizations.

For more than 25 years working in healthcare as management engineers, we have led teams in their attempts to improve profitability, quality, reliability, and service. In reality, we have witnessed many people spending the majority of their time stomping out fires. Any hopes that operations improvement projects (process improvement, total quality management [TQM], Continuous Quality Improvement [CQI], Six Sigma, Lean, and the list goes on) would create breakthrough transformations have been too frequently dashed by backsliding and phantom savings. The effort, energy, and resources that well-meaning organizations invest are more likely to lead to frustration than to success. The *Wall Street Journal* reports that 70% of process improvement projects fail, and our own experiences show that only half of healthcare improvement projects meet their objectives.[1]

This book provides a set of instructions to construct your departmental, divisional, or organizational functional tree structure (FTS) and work toward world-class service. The following chapters outline a method that will help your organization set a stable base for future improvements that are sustainable and create breakthrough improvements in service, quality, and costs. More important, the FTS method will provide you with the tools you need to build your processes tailored to your customer specifications and standards. It will enable you to improve your department, division, and entire organization and edge ahead of your competitors.

In the early chapters, we provide background that identifies our experiences with failed process improvements and the experiences of others. We wanted to confirm that we were not the only ones with problems. From talking to colleagues and administrators and sitting on panels at professional society meetings, we heard about plenty of successes, but even more failures (or, more accurately, partial successes). Later chapters illustrate our findings and demonstrate how to document your current processes, stabilize them, and optimize them to support long-term change. In addition, throughout the text you will find a wealth of diagnostic tools and assessment exercises that will help uncover your organization's functional deficits and chart the steps you can take to achieve organizational power and stability, the building blocks of successful long-term process improvement.

Finally, the information is intended to be a road map through a journey that will take patience and time. It is in our nature to see a problem and want to fix it. Unfortunately, more of the problems that we see are indicative of undocumented and unstable processes. "Fixing" these problems at best will be ineffective and at worst will have unintended poor consequences. Not only do we need to get to the root of the problem, but we also need to stabilize the process before building that solution.

Endnote

1. Chakravorty, Satya S. Where process-improvement projects go wrong. *Wall Street Journal*, January 25, 2010.

Chapter 1

Failure

As process consultants, too many of the improvements that we have tried to implement in healthcare failed. We came to understand, after a good deal of review, that they were built on the shifting sands of poorly documented processes carried out by well-meaning people in highly variable ways managed by people who did not always see enough of the picture. If errors and inefficiencies in healthcare surprise you, then you likely have not studied the frequently inconsistent, undocumented, wildly varying, and unfortunately, expensive industry we call the healthcare "system."*

From our vantage point, all healthcare organizations strive to improve the services they offer. They seek cost savings and compliance with regulations and guidelines. Every healthcare organization we have surveyed has commissioned process improvement teams and trained them to follow programs that have revolutionized the manufacturing industry, such as CQI (Continuous Quality Improvement), Plan-Do-Study-Act (PDSA)

---

* We cannot help but note the irony in the standard vernacular we use in explaining the provision of health as a healthcare "system" when we know that a *system* is "a set of principles or procedures according to which something is done; an organized scheme or method" (definition #2; 2014 Oxford University Press. Found at http://oxforddictionaries.com/us/definition/american_english/system?q=system).

cycle, Six Sigma, Lean, and Lean Six. Staff have been trained, scope statements written, and scorecards implemented. Despite these efforts, we were astounded by the number of projects that failed to meet their stated objectives and whose measures of success showed diminishing or no returns. Why would processes used so effectively in manufacturing fare so poorly in healthcare? Why have we not seen breakthrough improvements in costs and quality? The level of service has not increased as costs decreased—why? What keeps the healthcare industry from achieving the same improvements that we have seen documented in manufacturing?

These were the questions we asked as the early improvement projects we led produced disappointing long-term results. Trained as industrial engineers, we identified problems and measured their magnitude, found root causes, established buy-in from the cross-functional team on the proposed solution, carefully planned and documented the new methods, followed all of the project management steps, and measured the entire process. Conducting audits of completed projects a year later, we would find one of the following scenarios:

1. The team/department never fully implemented the proposed changes.
2. The proposed changes were made and then partially dismantled.
3. The proposed changes were in place but may have been the catalyst for additional or new problems in the department or in subsequent processes.
4. The proposed improvement suboptimized the next process or department, negating any benefits.
5. The proposed changes were made, and there were measurable lasting results.

To be honest, we did not often find that last scenario. In our debriefs of process improvement teams and process owners, we would frequently hear complaints that the team was not supported, that they did not have enough time to implement the proposed solutions, or that people, departments, administration, machines, or something else did not support the changes recommended. People would find numerous reasons why the proposed solution should not be implemented. Teams felt that the individuals were not supportive or did not care to change. Many hated the interruption to their current work processes. The bottom line, in the eyes of the team members and process owners, was that the proposed changes were either shortsighted or just would not work in their current environment.

We had to ask ourselves if we were wrong, if process improvement just could not work in healthcare the way it did in manufacturing. What was it about the healthcare environment that seemed so inhospitable to sustained improvement?

We set out on a journey to find the "root cause," to use the process improvement terminology of failure. To be fair, we knew that all process improvement projects did not end in failure; it was just that too many of them only marginally improved the process or had sustained success. Through our review of teams and interviews with their members, we began to see common effects but not root causes. Our initial Ishikowa diagram looked like Figure 1.1.

The outcomes were easy to identify, but the root causes eluded us. We began to look at common causes that were evident in every project that failed to create sustained improvements. The flaws that we frequently saw were

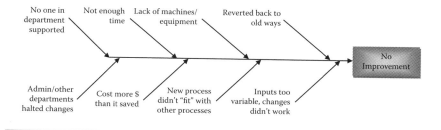

Figure 1.1   Ishikowa diagram of root causes of failures for process improvements.

piecemeal approaches to selecting projects, projects started in areas that lacked standardization or existed in an environment already plagued by complex problems, and projects that solved a local problem but did not meet the specifications of the next process. The project teams were trying to build solutions to problems that existed in environments that were not stable, optimized, and aligned.

Still, it is overly simple to think that process improvements will automatically take hold if implemented in a stable, optimized, and aligned environment because there is one more lesson that we serendipitously learned. Ask anyone working in a hospital what their job is and they can give you a pretty specific rundown of everything that they do. They most likely can give you information about the processes that feed their process and *may* know something about the process that follows their process. Unfortunately, their worldview is limited to the process in their area (Figure 1.2). They may understand the processes in their department but may not understand the

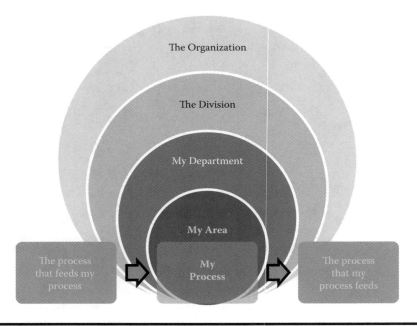

Figure 1.2 Understanding "my process."

previous or future processes in the department. Furthermore, if two people are doing the same job in the same area of a hospital, it is highly likely that both would provide a different explanation of the process they take. In fact, it is likely that every individual would describe and handle their process differently from everyone else. We have found this to be the case frequently when interviewing staff on the work process that they follow on simple procedures. This variation in process likely leads to variation in the level of quality and even failures in the goods or services created. It also is most certainly more costly.

Most people working in healthcare have a limited view and understanding of the entire process. This is as true for the janitor cleaning floors as it is in the C-suite.* Sometimes, we have been amused at the level of understanding that a janitor has compared to those running the business. The lack of standard, uniform processes and a conceptual model of how all processes fit together in an organization hinders the ability to make lasting changes. What improves my process may hinder your process. Many organizations have tried to assist employees in understanding their organization by reiterating the mission, vision, and guiding principles. There is nothing wrong with this, but it still does not get to the issue of why process improvement projects fail to provide lasting or breakthrough improvements.

Much of this insight was brought to light by an innocent question posed by the newly hired chief financial officer (CFO), who was perplexed over the complexity of our hospital and hospital system. He had come from a 30-year career in banking, and this was his first foray into healthcare.

He asked us to create a flow chart of the *entire* hospital process, from admission to discharge to billing to collections. With enough time and large sheets of paper, we knew it could

---

* A term encompassing the executives of an organization (e.g., the CEO, COO, CFO, CIO, CMO, and so on).

be done. Yet, as "process experts," we realized that even we did not have a reasonable understanding of the entire process or the individual processes that roll up to the "entire" process. Worse yet, our administrators did not understand the entire process. Did they need to? To make breakthrough and lasting improvements, the answer is Yes, at least in their area, the preceding suppliers, and the customers of the goods that their process provides.

You may ask whether it is feasible to understand the entire process, especially processes as complicated as those in hospitals, hospital systems, or healthcare organizations. Hospitals are without question dynamic and complicated systems. Creating a flowchart of the processes that run an entire hospital would not provide our CFO the understanding that he needed. At one level, it would be too complicated to work with, yet the process needed to be understood intimately by someone in the production process. Our first step was to create a method to visualize the entire system so that management could support process improvements. We called this creating "functional tree structures" (FTSs). At first glance, an FTS diagram looks like an organizational chart, and it does help to show the different functions within a department, hospital, and division. But, it concisely provides more information as well. It breaks down a department into functions and then processes and helps to portray the magnitude of each function's outputs. It shows the building blocks or DNA of a department, hospital, or division. It does not dwell on who is running each function, which is immaterial; it helps to visualize what is done. And, it is simple to create. We return to this concept in Chapter 5.

Our second insight into why healthcare process improvement projects frequently failed was not as simple. The largest difference between improvement projects in manufacturing and healthcare was the state of the current process prior to implementing an improvement. We came to the realization that process had to be in a relatively stable state. We had to remove as much variability in the environment as possible—to standardize and optimize individual processes. Once this was accomplished, we could begin to review how well each of the processes and their inputs and outputs aligned. The projects that did not meet expectations, reverted to their preimprovement inefficiencies, or just failed always tried to improve on something that was unstable; the process improvement project did nothing to address the instability. These are classic "Band-Aid" projects. Issues were identified and measured, solutions created, and project plans initiated. And, in six months, the issues had not been solved, and quality was no better. What became evident was that before lasting improvements could be made, the process needed to be stable. For the outcomes to be stable, the inputs and process had to be uniform and standardized—within acceptable tolerances, much like processes in manufacturing, but this was rarely the case in healthcare.

To convey to others what we meant by *stable*, we came up with a simple acronym that fit not only what had to be done but also easily explained the steps needed to achieve a stable process. The acronym is SOAP. We needed departments and the organization as a whole to standardize, optimize, and align their processes. When a hospital or even a department or part of a department standardizes, optimizes, and aligns its processes, it has a stable process.

We did find one example of a healthcare organization that already understood this. Small, specialized surgicenters were making money hand over fist because they understood this principle. They had the advantage of doing only a limited number of things, but they did them efficiently: they had a standardized, optimized, aligned process. To compete in this environment and be profitable, hospitals need to become as stable.

After trying to implement the concepts of Lean and Six Sigma in the mid-1990s, we became frustrated with the failure rate of most of these approaches. These process improvement concepts did not seem to work for the process improvement teams. As discussed previously, they addressed issues but tried to implement improvements on unstable processes. The concepts focused on improvements, and the methods used are effective, but they are most effective making improvements on processes whose core is stable. What they ignored was the variation in how processes were performed and linked. We felt that they were ineffective in displaying the entire process and answering the key questions of what, how, who, where, and how long when documenting a process and understanding each activity.

We tinkered with different ways of displaying how a process and the underlying functions work and eventually developed a hybrid tool that documented the what, how, who, where, and how long of the entire hospital's current processes. We started by documenting the current state of operations for each department. This is especially important when deploying new technology or a new process, as the tool helps visualize the influence of the new technology on each process and makes the gap between the before and after states visible, tangible, and easy to understand.

Everything did not work at first. We overlooked the importance of building improvements on a stable set of processes. At the beginning, departments were happy with the outcomes of projects that used our visual tools. The operating room (OR) liked the new room turnover times, and nursing units appreciated the transportation team's responsiveness. Despite this, most of the improvements began to fade six to nine months after deployment. Even though we established a performance measurement system that tracked carefully developed metrics, the process improvements reverted to their prior practice, and advancements evaporated. Frustrated, we spent the next four years modifying and perfecting the tools and methods to make them universal for any process evaluation in many hospital departments. The primary goal was to help departments and teams achieve lasting success by improving operations and enhancing customers' satisfaction. These enhanced tools and concepts became FTSs.

A few years later, while working with the hospital's environmental services (EVS) ("housekeeping") department, we realized that there was something even more fundamental in creating lasting change. EVS was the scapegoat for every nursing unit's discharge and inpatient bed assignment problems, generating an outsize amount of grumbling at every staff meeting. Despite relatively high efficiency and effectiveness, the department could not keep up with the discharge process at every hour of every day. To address these issues, we worked with the department to develop a monitoring system that should have addressed the department staffing patterns and demand. We made modifications to the current scheduling and room-cleaning prioritization processes. Although at first the changes appeared to help, as time progressed, it became obvious that the new processes were not going to create lasting improvements. The scheduling and prioritization process seemed to help EVS, but this was not the only department in the process. This department's changes improved what was happening in EVS but did not help the service it was providing the customer, the nursing unit.

We needed to review the entire process to determine where the system was breaking down. Using FTS and current-state mapping with EVS, we immediately helped the department to see what the other departments were complaining about and helped EVS communicate within and outside the department the misalignments, inefficiencies, bottlenecks, and instabilities within the process. From here, we studied all of the processes within the department at a more microlevel and how they fit into the procedures of the department's customers, namely, nursing. Our goal was to improve the timeliness and quality of the bed assignment process with changes that would sustain the results and engage the staff. Not only did we find inefficiencies and bottlenecks within the department, but also we identified inconsistencies with what we call our "inputs," which led to variability in our "outputs." The diagrams and analyses we generated made it apparent to all that the entire process had flaws and was unstable. We did not have the luxury of being able to reengineer the entire process. It is generally impossible to dismantle and rebuild a process that needs to continue in a living hospital. Just as a heart surgeon has to work on a body that needs to continue running, we needed to employ a process that allowed us to see and communicate the issues, stabilize the process, make corrections, sew up the patient, and monitor closely initially and then at regular intervals for any changes.

After completing the FTS process with EVS, room availability for new patients increased (the number of rooms waiting to be cleaned before a new patient could be admitted). We have gone on to refine the tool, taking out unneeded steps, adding steps that we realized helped, simplifying, documenting, and experimenting until we came up with the process we now apply.

The FTS helps to delineate the what and how of every process that is conducted at the functional, departmental, divisional, and organizational levels. Until all staff at every level (subprocess, process, subfunction, function, department, division, and organization) understand *what* they are doing (the objective and how it fits with other processes) and *how* they are doing it (eliminating variation between staff members and between the first time and the last time a process is done in a day), lasting improvements are unlikely. Yet, this is only the first step. The next step is to focus on standardizing processes and reducing variation within and between operators and departments. If a department has ten technicians, then all ten should deliver the same sequence of activities and events that result in exactly the same service. They should be able to define their contributions to the final product and connect their process to those in their department, division, and organization as well as link their role to the strategic plan, mission, and vision of the organization.

Imagine this: Your staff in every department understand the FTS for their area and work to standardize, optimize, and align every process. Would not the elimination of poor quality and savings in time, duplicate effort, litigation costs, and headaches more than pay for the effort required to realign your healthcare system? How can you get to the point that everyone in your organization is "doing it right the first time"?

Chapter 2

Defining and Delivering Quality in Healthcare

Introduction

Theoretically, "How can a hospital provide quality?" is a simple question. Practically, it is not so simple to answer. Classic definitions focus on providing what the customer desires. Every person and every process have customers. Some are internal, such as the physician who orders a test or procedure, and some are external, such as the patient or the patient's insurance company. If quality is providing the desired outcome, then we need to focus on creating products or services that, at a minimum, conform to customers' desires. Still, this does not answer the question of how that will occur. We all know that most employees at a hospital want to provide what the customer desires, but sometimes they are constrained by processes that keep them from delivering on this desire.

The next "logical" step is to commission a quality improvement team to "improve quality," and after four months of meetings and six months of backsliding, the level of quality is no better than where it started ten months before. The quality improvement process may have been carried out correctly. But, quality improvement does not guarantee better quality. The improvement process may be solid, but the process being improved could be unstable. It is important to understand that *quality* and *quality improvement* are two completely separate concepts.

Quality occurs when there is consistent conformance to desired standards. The level of quality is a measure of a product's or service's consistent conformance to desired standards. Measurable outputs include nurse response time or a clear ultrasound exam. In sports, manufacturing, and services, high performance comes where there is high conformance. The free-throw shooter with the highest percentage of baskets likely practices every day and follows the same rules and rituals. The most reliable product is built to the highest level of *consistency*. In its heyday, Bell Telephone built the most reliable telephones. They were not feature laden, but they consistently worked, never broke down, never ran out of power, were built to withstand harsh treatment, and could easily last 20 years. Today's cell phones certainly cannot make these claims.

Quality improvement is changing the process or improving the inputs that make up the product or service. You cannot improve simply by doing the same thing. A major league batter in a hitting slump will review his stance, the placement of his feet, the grip on the bat, or the weight or length of the bat and make adjustments. Likewise, when ultrasound scans are consistently fuzzy or misaligned, the ultrasound technician can review the procedures and equipment and develop, communicate, and implement a new procedure.

Whenever we have process variation and continuously changing inputs, the output will vary. This is the antithesis of quality. If workers accept that some x-rays will need to be redone or that results from a laboratory test will return to the nursing unit some time between 15 minutes and 8 hours, then quality suffers. Accepting process variation and wide variation in inputs produces erratic outputs at best. Should a caregiver accept low-quality inputs and should management accept wide variations in a process? Or, worse yet, should a department build its process knowing that the previous process provides inputs that are unpredictable or of varying levels of quality?

Each customer in a string of processes has standards for the product they receive. Conformance to their standard not only improves their satisfaction but also improves the quality of the subsequent process. If results from a certain laboratory test generally are returned to the primary care physician in one hour, but 25% of the tests come in two or more hours, the physician subconsciously becomes trained to expect all of the tests to come in two hours and acts accordingly, slowing down and potentially harming a patient. Or, if the physician expects the results in one hour but by the luck of the draw does not receive results for three hours, the physician and the patient will be disappointed with the response time and care received.

One classic example is a case of discharge summary transcription turnaround time at a large suburban hospital. The director of medical records proudly explained that the average discharge summary turnaround time was within the standard of 24 hours (Figure 2.1). After the summary was dictated, the physicians had to review and approve the summary before the patient's insurance could be billed. While the medical records director was proud of the accomplishment, the physicians were dissatisfied. Indeed, while the average was less than 24 hours (23 hours to be exact), 48% of the time, physicians received the summaries after 24 hours. The medical records director misunderstood the expectations of the physicians and what they saw as the acceptable standard. The physicians wanted the summaries ready for their review within 24 hours, not within an *average* of 24 hours. The wide variation in output did not meet the customers' (in this case, physicians') expectations of quality and suboptimized the next phase of discharge planning by significantly delaying the insurance-billing process.

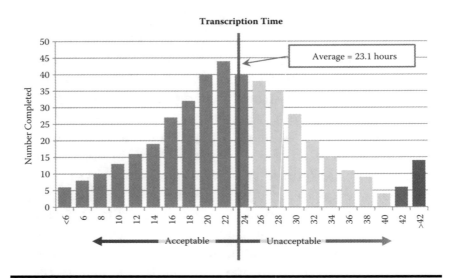

Figure 2.1   Average or expected transcription time.

This brings us to the second goal in defining quality. Variation in any aspect of the product or service is generally thought of as not meeting the quality expectations. If you went to a coffee shop and ordered a double mocha latte and received a Coke—which has the same number of calories and the same number of ounces—you would not be satisfied. The barista may have conformed to the standard of something to drink that is sweet and at the correct volume but he missed other important expectations. Similarly, if each time you went in and ordered a double mocha latte and the cost changed every day, the variation would not be considered quality. If some days the coffee is hot and other days cold, you would not believe that you were getting consistent service. If it was sweet one day and bitter the next, it would not meet your expectations.

Conformance to a standard *on average* or *in principle* is not quality. But, reducing variation, even if you do not meet your customers' expectations, improves the customers' perceptions. Processes that minimize variation provide a more reliable product and measurable quality. Furthermore, quality improvements cannot occur unless there is minimal variation—conformance to standards—and therefore a stable structure.

Aren't We Already Providing the Highest Level of Healthcare Possible?

Healthcare organizations in the United States frequently suffer from the belief that they are doing most everything right. Advertisements and slogans would have us believe that there is no need to change when everything is going so well:

■ "We provide the highest possible quality to our patients."
■ "We are the best in our community."
■ "We are the most caring organization."
■ "Our people are the best."

If any of these statements honestly described the health organization, then maybe they would have a chance at long-term sustainability. Truth be told, the mantra of most is more like, "We've been doing this for many years, so why should we change it now?" This belief is exactly what will lead to eventual failure.

Healthcare is probably the last major industry (and it is a major industry, consuming one in six dollars of the gross domestic product [GDP]) to embrace highly effective electronic communications and the use of continuous, sustainable, process improvement. Yet, electronic medical records and Continuous Quality Improvement (CQI) will not ensure sustainability. For every CQI success story, how many project restarts, project failures, and project abandonments are there? Did the project hold gains for any substantial period of time?

Continued success requires that an organization evolve from a "learned institution" to a "learning institution." It must begin from a known and stable starting point, requiring a deep understanding of its systems and processes, before successful change can be implemented. What we are suggesting is that *improvements made to a **stable process** pave the way for **additional improvements***. Improvements in process, materials, and labor lead to profitability, and you are no doubt reading this book because you are unsatisfied with your hospital's or healthcare organization's capacity to improve in one or all of these arenas.

By definition, a great process is a set of sequenced activities and tasks that provides consistent and excellent results. To develop great processes requires detailed "engineering" activities similar to those introduced to healthcare in the 1920s by Frank and Lillian Gilbreth. Using early industry techniques like ergonomics and time and motion studies, the Gilbreths attempted to simplify the processes and decrease stress and error for hospital staff. In the 1970s, as competition began to heat up, hospitals started employing the knowledge, skills, and tools of the industrial engineers (often referred to as management engineers) to increase efficiency, reduce error, and improve the quality of services. Difficulty finding trained management engineers led to hospitals hiring individuals with business and consulting experience. Although not intimately comfortable using engineering tools and concepts, these individuals were able to follow and administer the basic engineering techniques with some business school flair. Whether something was lost in the translation between engineering principles and management techniques is debatable. What is not is the need for improvement and the use of industry-tested tools to improve hospital processes.

We would like to challenge healthcare organizations to think in a new way. In learning organizations, there are no impediments to new and better opportunities for improving services or products. Certainly, there are large, bureaucratic organizations that appear to survive, but are they flourishing? In most cases, these organizations are missing opportunities, losing energetic and creative staff, and in worst cases, losing customers. If anyone in an organization believes that their processes are at their highest level of efficiency and producing a unique, unrivaled product, then the organization is in peril.

In successful companies, improvement is the primary responsibility of management. We pay managers to bring about change, not to manage people, manage processes, produce quarterly earnings, or provide a public face for the company. The most important role in any organization is process monitoring and process management, not personnel or departmental management. Change creates new ideas, better ideas, innovations, and improvements. Did Apple stop improving the iPod even though it was common belief that it was the best personal music system available?

Put another way, good is the enemy of the great. Palm Pilots and BlackBerrys, once the unchallenged favorites of power users and personal assistants alike, fell prey to changes in the marketplace and watched their market share and stock decline. No doubt they were good, but something great came along. Not coincidentally, Apple's iPhone was the device to edge out BlackBerry's dominance in the business handset arena.

Competition, environmental and governmental requirements, and process drift underscore the crucial need to continuously improve. Maintaining the status quo is equivalent to a slow death. The focus and mindset of everyone in an organization must be on improving the products and services provided. The alternative can be found in the Palm Pilots of the healthcare industry: hospitals that failed to nimbly address changes in the competitive environment, that once owned their community market but were closed or merged, or that produced poor outcomes and became not only economically unviable but also dangerous. Yet, even in organizations where process improvement is the mantra, we see some process improvement failures and many projects for which the projected outcomes far exceed the actual outcomes. But, why?

In service organizations like hospitals, the largest input into a process is staff, yet common management techniques tend to alienate rather than motivate staff. Creating internal competition through poorly administered management-by-objectives programs and individual- or departmental-level rewards undermines everyone's performance. Success in service organizations depends on teamwork, where the team is everyone, not departments, not divisions, not vice presidents, not C-suite executives. Success becomes impossible when individuals become disenfranchised and unengaged. On top of that, unstable, unaligned, and suboptimized processes create chaotic conditions, and lack of training and administrative support makes it impossible to deliver service consistency and process excellence.

But, let us be clear. Although an organization's most reliable ingredient for success lies in its staff, process improvement failures come from a host of reasons. If we were to use one of the most elemental tools in process improvement, the Ishikawa diagram, and chart the root causes of failures and then use the tried-and-true Pareto principle, we would find that process improvement failure is built on *process instability* (Figure 2.2).

Instability is fostered in large part by not understanding when, how, and why a process is working. It is rare in healthcare that a department director can explain in detail the major functions of the department and enumerate the resources that have been devoted to each function. Equally rare is the director who can provide a quick summary of the department functions, subfunctions, processes, and associated activities tasks. As a result, functional overlap, duplication of efforts, and competing priorities across departments are rampant, often causing error and dissatisfaction for the department customer or patient.

One area in which hospital departments most obviously encounter friction rather than coordination is in finances. Each unit functions within a separate budget, guaranteeing that

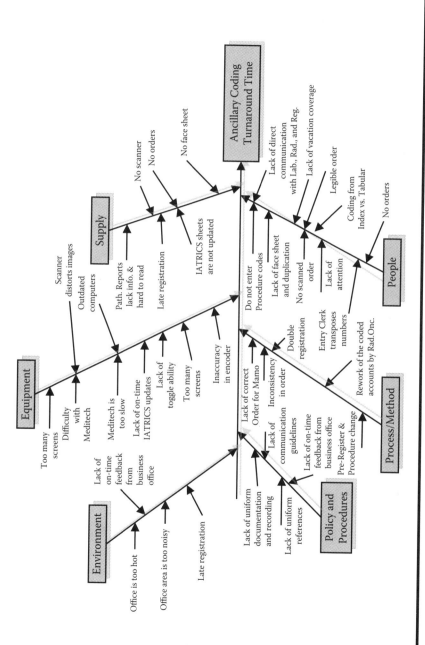

Figure 2.2   Root causes of instability in ancillary coding.

operations are dictated not by customer demand but by a set of numbers that constrain functional expansion or contraction and ignore the deep connections among discrete departments. In this operational environment, separate (and now competing) departments cannot function as a homogeneous system. For example, many emergency departments (EDs) will stack patients who need to be admitted to a nursing floor in the hallways of the ED. The nursing units frequently delay new admissions because they require a significant amount of time to go through the standard admitting processes, sometimes hoping that the new patient is then admitted on the next shift. This is not because the nurse is uncaring or lazy. If a medical/surgical nurse is assigned five patients and currently has four and an empty bed, that nurse may feel that the 35 to 45 minutes required to admit a new patient while other patients may need care would reduce the nurse's ability to care for the other four patients. The nursing unit's actions suboptimizes the ED. If the demand is high, one possible solution would be to have a floating admitting nurse who would go to all nursing units to process and admit the patient to the floor, freeing the ED and the unit nurse and providing better care.

Silo-based structures are vulnerable to inconsistent and incoherent communication across functional areas, reducing staff engagement, sabotaging opportunity for collaboration, and increasing the probability of introducing errors. Some of the country's leading hospitals have blazed a remarkable trail by breaking down the silo structure and truly integrating once-fragmented departmental operations. A perfect example of this was an ancillary coding department that was receiving incomplete charts from admitting, radiology, and the laboratory. The coders were completing, on average, 72 charts per hour, and data entry clerks had to input the codes they created. Much of the coders' time was spent calling doctors' offices to obtain missing information. On review, we found that 30% of the charts arrived to the ancillary coding department incomplete. The ancillary coding department went to the admitting, radiology, and laboratory departments and trained the registration clerks on the data that should be captured. Remarkably, the registration clerks had never been told of the specific criteria and data needed for a complete chart. Within one month, 95% of the charts arriving to the ancillary coding department were complete. The coders were now coding 125 charts per hour and were entering the data directly into the system, thus saving the time of the data entry clerks. In a "siloed" organization, this type of interaction rarely occurs, and processes are not aligned and optimized. A simple innovation—education—solved a costly problem for the ancillary coding department and all of the doctors' offices that had to provide information after the fact.

Stability might be the last characteristic you would assign to your hospital or to the healthcare industry in general. Amid new market conditions and competitors, shifting regulatory and credentialing requirements, increased and sometimes unpredictable patient demands, and likely a parade of consultants offering you a host of out-of-the-box solutions to manage it all, you may feel lost at sea as you face a turbulent and ever-changing healthcare market. The rest of this book develops the core principles that will guide you in developing an organizational culture that is primed for sustainable quality improvement.

The following are the core principles we prescribe:

■ *Make the process visible.* If you cannot "see" how a product is being produced, you will not be able to identify opportunities for errors and process variation. When processes are documented and visible, their outputs are more likely to be stable and will meet customers' expectations.
■ *Be honest.* Do not defend poor procedures and bad outcomes. Realize the need for change and understand that lasting change only occurs on improvements built on stable processes.
■ *Standardize.* The act of standardization identifies unneeded variations in a process. It also reveals any tasks

done in conjunction with the process that have little, if any, value to the end customer.

- *Align.* Align processes and incentives with customers' needs and requirements.
- *Understand.* Understand workload trends and high-demand periods and use heuristic staffing models to meet customer demands.
- *Stabilize.* Before any improvement begins, the process being improved must be in a stable state. There should be only a minimum amount of random variation in the outputs of the process before any lasting improvements can be attempted.
- *Learn the right tools.* The core body of knowledge and skills used in process improvement is wasted on unstable processes. A new body of knowledge, skills, and training is required for healthcare leaders to make lasting change.
- *Manage change.* The best managers manage change prospectively. This includes changes in the environment, changes in demand, changes in inputs, and the list continues. Foster an entrepreneurial approach at all levels but do not eliminate stable processes unless they no longer meet customer needs.
- *Improve.* Only after you have a standardized, optimized, aligned process can you begin on process improvement.

Armed with these guiding principles, hospitals and care facilities will thrive even in a difficult business environment. You will develop a vision that distinguishes your services from those of your competitors and locates excellence in all work processes. The core message of this book is that quality must be rooted in stable operations. You must first understand, and then standardize, optimize, and align all of your organization's processes before you can pursue lasting quality improvement. Your competitive edge is only as sharp as your functional processes; the following chapters illustrate specific methods for sharpening that edge.

Chapter 3

Phantom Successes

Introduction

Our experience in helping departments and teams improve their processes led us to question whether all of the effort made in improving processes in healthcare was to anyone's benefit. Anecdotal comments and experiences from colleagues only supported our concerns. We could easily come up with a list of why certain projects failed to meet their objectives or why some projects failed before they ever got to the implementation phase. What we did notice was the difficulty colleagues had in creating lasting improvements. One joke common in consulting and management engineering is, "If we made lasting improvements [or "If they ever implemented our recommendations"], then we would all be out of jobs." We frequently found ourselves called back to improve processes in a department a year after we thought the issue had been solved by the prior process improvement project.

To understand more about the success rate of process improvement projects, we reached out to professionals in the process improvement community with a short survey. Our objective was to identify whether project success and sustainability were the norm or whether improvements in healthcare did not meet the levels of success often found in manufacturing. In addition, we wanted their opinions on the primary reasons for project shortcomings and failures. Our hypothesis was that we were not the only organization for which process improvement did not always end up improving the process. We wanted to obtain a healthcare industry read on project failure and whether it was as dismal as some have estimated, including a *Wall Street Journal* study noting the "brutal fact" that the low success rate of initiatives such as new technology, downsizing, restructuring, or changing corporate culture contributes to an overall change initiative failure rate of 70%.[*]

Although our findings are directional and in no means scientific in scope or size, they do confirm what others have surmised: Process improvement projects are not always successful. Using our connections with healthcare societies, we sent out a survey to over 400 professionals involved with process improvements in healthcare. We surveyed stakeholders, champions, process owners, project leaders, facilitators, team members, and support analysts who had taken part in a process improvement project in a healthcare facility in the previous two years. In total, we based our conclusions on responses from 110 people whose focus was in the healthcare field and who had been directly involved in process improvements.

Although less bleak than a 70% failure rate, these responses still showed that half of the process improvement projects failed to meet some or all of their stated goals: Half (49%) were deemed successful, about a third were somewhat successful, and one in six (16%) was deemed unsuccessful (Figure 3.1).

Even the projects that were successful did not always have sustained gains. Health process improvement professionals cited that half of the somewhat and completely successful projects could not maintain their gains for more than one

---

[*] Chakravorty, Satya S., Where Process-Improvement Projects Go Wrong, *Wall Street Journal*, January 25, 2010.

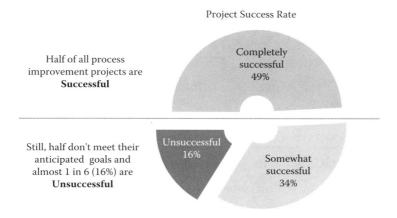

Figure 3.1   Process improvement project success rate.

year. Similar to our own experiences, many of the projects that began with what appeared to be promising changes could not maintain the gains projected for the new process. Environments change, people forget, monitoring is not followed through, new equipment breaks, and a number of other things happen, and the gains made and expected from a process improvement project begin to evaporate. For us, what was most surprising was the percentage of evaporation. Within a year, only half (51%) of the projects that were deemed a success kept their improvements (Figure 3.2).

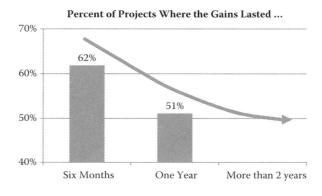

Figure 3.2   Process improvement project gain backsliding.

	Maintained Gains	
	% maintained their gains for at least six (6) months	% maintained their gains for more than one year
Unsuccessful	57%	43%
Successful	70%	63%
All	62%	51%

Figure 3.3   Backsliding for successful and unsuccessful projects.

We further segmented the participants into those who felt that more than half of their institution's process improvement projects were successful (the "successful") and those who felt that more than half or their institution's projects were unsuccessful (the "unsuccessful"). Even the successful group found that only three of five (63%) of the projects were able to sustain their gains for more than 12 months, leaving two of five (37%) to experience backsliding. The participants whose experience led them to say that half or more of their organization's projects were unsuccessful reported that only 43% were able to sustain their gains for over a year (Figure 3.3).

We queried further into the lack of successes of process improvement projects in hopes to refine our understanding of the attributes needed for achieving lasting gains in quality. We first focused on the mechanics of process improvement programs by asking: *If one or more of the projects you have been involved with were not completely successful, what were the primary factors or reasons that the process improvement projects did not reach their potential benefits?*

Reasons Projects Did Not Reach Their Potential Benefits

With colleagues, we had brainstormed reasons that projects were not able to reach and maintain their potential. As would be expected, lack of commitment to the solution by management, the departments involved with the process, stakeholders, or others was frequently cited as an issue faced by process improvement teams. Basically, it is not in the nature of humans to embrace change in their work environments. Most people will complain about their work environment and will go so far as to explain their solution to the problems they encounter or observe. Yet, it is quite another thing to embrace and sustain change. We came up with a dozen reasons for project failure. Our brainstormed reasons for failure seemed reliable, but we wanted to sample a larger group of process improvement professionals.

We asked participants in our survey to rate whether these likely failure factors highly influenced the failures of a process improvement project they were involved with, moderately influenced, or had no influence on the failure. Again, issues associated with lack of support from management and departmental stakeholders were the most frequently cited reasons for failure. The issues that had little or no effect on failure included lack of use for the process improvement tools and techniques, untrained or unknowledgeable facilitators and team members, and demand from the customer for an improvement (Figure 3.4).

We dug further into the data to review the ratings given by those who primarily had successful teams compared to those whose process improvement projects were more likely to be unsuccessful and found that the ratings were comparable. On only two measures, *low team engagement or other problems with team structure* and *project goals and plans were not adequate*, did the two groups differ. Both of these issues would certainly keep a process improvement team from being successful. Unclear or inadequate plans and goals mean that the team had little direction, which could lead to low team engagement or having the wrong people on the team. More important is that the ratings of reasons for failure were *similar* for organizations that generally had successful teams and those that generally had unsuccessful teams. This suggests

If one or more of the projects with which you have been involved were not completely successful, what were the primary factors or reasons that the process improvement projects did not reach their potential benefits?

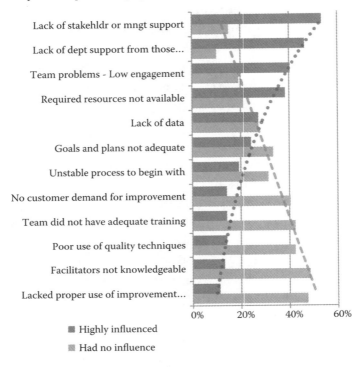

Figure 3.4   Factors in process improvement failures.

that tools and techniques are not to blame for the unsuccessful outcomes of process improvements (Figure 3.5).

Issues that Highly Influenced a Process Improvement Team's Lack of Success and Sustainment

As mentioned, respondents clearly identified a lack of management, stakeholder, and departmental support as the leading cause of process improvement failure. Why would departments involved with the process being improved not support

Ratings from organizations where more than half of the projects were	Successful	Not Successful
Lack of stakeholder or management support	50%	55%
Lack of support from departments involved in the process	43%	48%
Low team engagement - problems with team structure	30%	47%
Required resources were not available	38%	38%
Lack of data on the area being improved	30%	25%
Project goals and plans were not adequate	18%	28%
Unstable process to begin with	20%	18%
Lack of customer or regulatory demand for improvement	10%	17%
Team members did not have adequate training or skills	15%	13%
Poor use of techniques (6 Sigma, Lean, CQI, etc.)	13%	15%
Facilitators were not knowledgeable	13%	13%
Lack of proper use of improvement tools	8%	13%

Figure 3.5   Influencers in process improvement success.

a process improvement project? After all, they would share in the savings and enjoy some of the improvements as well. Certainly, the fear of change and the general unwillingness to embrace change make some people reluctant to make improvements. But, we also wondered whether there was something deeper that was not being addressed.

This question led directly to the hypothesis we were developing about unstable processes sabotaging quality improvement efforts. In talking with those on the front lines of implementing the recommendations of a process improvement project, the fear of change was not what we observed. Improvements that were abandoned or only partially implemented did not seem to fit. Whether the change was forced on them or they were part of the team's "solution," some recommendations did not make sense to staff charged with implementing them or the solutions hindered other parts of the entire process. Proposed changes that do not account for the nuances and complexity of the process being "improved" run the risk of implementing change that stakeholders cannot and will not support.

Everyone in healthcare knows that servicing patients is not always easy. The variability in the patients, doctors, conditions, secondary complicating conditions, laws, insurance rules, and so on make for a dynamic environment. Often, our solutions were the best we had to offer given what we knew. Intuitively, the frontline workers knew that our solutions were not optimal. Their managers, especially those who had firsthand or previous work experience, probably sensed the disconnects and could not wholeheartedly support the changes recommended. It should be no surprise, then, that the supposed gains had evaporated by the 6- or 12-month mark, if not immediately.

As department directors, process improvement team leaders, or management engineers, we were certainly guilty of building solutions while not being fully aware of the underlying processes. Our job was to show proposed savings and improved patient outcomes. Actual savings were "outside our control," and handling the nuances was the department's responsibility. We had new projects to attend to, and taking the time to review the underlying structure of the department was a luxury that did not at first appear to be a crucial step in the quality improvement process.

The end result is sadly predictable. Solutions built on top of unstable structures fail. The employees in the process knew that something was not right. The variability in the outputs and outcomes of the process would suggest that something in the inputs or the process itself led to this variability. Creating improvements that would be placed over an unstable structure would invite failure. Projects in these circumstances had nowhere to go but to crumble under their own weight.

More telling was the responses to the open ended question: *What were the primary factors or reasons that the process improvement projects did not reach their potential benefits?*

The group with primarily successful projects discussed lack of administrative support, process issues with the process improvement process, and a lack of dedicated resources for those projects that failed to meet expectations. The unsuccessful group also had these reasons, but the biggest issue they had was categorized into a lack of a standardized, optimized, and aligned process at the beginning. This issue did not come up for those who had generally good outcomes for their projects. We did not ask for any measures of project success—just whether they met their predefined goals. The unsuccessful group stood out in that the projects they worked with began with an unstable base with operations and processes that were not standardized, optimized, and aligned.

Drivers of Success

If one or more of the projects you have been involved with were not completely successful, what were the primary factors or reasons that the process improvement projects did not reach their potential benefits (Figure 3.6)? Respondents' comments speak to the issues that we trace to a lack of a standardized, optimized, and aligned process. In the following list, participants' comments are in regular typeface and ours are in *italics*:

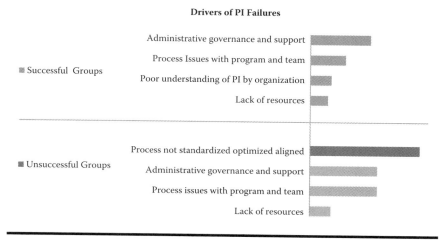

Figure 3.6   Drivers of process improvement failures.

"The process itself was not true therefore those involved did not buy into it." *This identifies a misaligned process.*

"Lack of complete current state process map and workflow analyses." *Without understanding the process, it is highly likely that the process is not standardized, optimized, and aligned.*

"Analysis of new process not done well and variation occurred." *When processes are not standardized, then variation will occur.*

"New process did not help the end user or resulted in more work." *This suggests a process that was both not aligned and not optimized.*

"Other processes outside of the scope of the effort had major failures resulting in a rollback (in one instance) to the prior process for the department." *This was likely the result of a misaligned process.*

"There wasn't enough confidence [experience] with the new process for the department to continue with it under the 'emergency' circumstances." *The new process was not optimized and likely required more work than the old process.*

"Implementation and sustainability are the key issues—trying to do TOO much." *Again, processes that are not standardized and optimized require additional effort.*

"MUCH more prep work should be done to identify and vet the understandable and measureable returns to convince folks the project was worth doing." *Without a thorough understanding of the process, it is impossible to create a lasting improvement. Basically, it means that the changes are built on an unstable process.*

"Staff overwhelmed and didn't take the time to follow through." *When staff are overwhelmed, it can identify improper staffing levels and processes that are inefficient, through suboptimization, misalignment, or built-in variability in the process—a lack of standardization.*

"Previous practice patterns were understood by all; new patterns of workflows are too difficult for all to remember."

The new patterns of workflows are likely not standardized and optimized.

"People leading the process didn't understand the processes to begin with." *You cannot fix what is not known.*

"Heavy workload on staff made it difficult to get them to change their processes." *Again, issues associated with staff not able to keep up with the workload suggest inefficient and misaligned processes and affords an opportunity to realign and standardize the process.*

"Holding staff accountable for process changes, keeping up with education, re-evaluating process changes, ¼ keeping team members involved." *Lacks administrative governance and support.*

"The scope too narrow and focused on one program versus whole process." *Working on one process and not focusing on the entire network of processes does not create lasting improvements.*

"Inability to tactically react to changes when required and true alignment with end point customer deliverables." *Unstable processes create a continuous supply of changes that must result in a reaction. Improvements can never be developed, much less become sustainable, in this environment. Improvement only comes after stabilization.*

These statements identify what is really the root cause of the majority of failures in process improvement projects. They describe the effects of processes that need to be reviewed and reworked at a deeper level. The processes need to be standardized, optimized, and aligned.

To further understand whether our thesis that failed improvement projects were built on top of unstable processes, we returned to personally interview a number of healthcare managers, Six Sigma experts, process improvement team members, and others who were involved with a failed process improvement team in the previous two years. What they told us confirmed that lack of success and failure to maintain gains came when projects were built on unstable processes. We next summarize some of their comments to make this point.

- What are the underlying causes of projects that do not provide lasting improvements?

  "The focus is *not* on the patient and family or customer."

  "Staff and physicians are *not* engaged, especially when the staff designs the new process(es)."

  "Standards are *not* implemented and checking and coaching *do not* occur."

  "The process owner and sponsor *do not* hold staff accountable for following standard work."

  "The staff is *not* encouraged to be continual problem solvers and not encouraged to learn."

- How would you describe the preproject environment in a successful project?

  "Pre-project environments for successful improvement projects have leaders who truly understand the effort that process improvement requires and hold everyone accountable for results."

  "Staff members must be trained to be problem solvers and are coached to ask the right questions to determine the root cause of an issue and develop the solutions."

  "The team engages team members and users, understands the Voice of the Customer, develops a detailed workflow of the current process, conducts a detailed gap analysis, ensures end users' support, and monitors progress to catch issues early."

- Examples of an implemented project that failed to meet the goals:

  Project: Laboratory order entry

  Reasons for failure: The executive leader told the team to focus on just one site, which created chaos since the individual lab sites were not able to send orders between different locations and submit charges to be paid. In addition, there was

poorly designed information technology infra-
structure. In the end, the executive leader's mis-
understanding of the tools, means, and processes
created additional chaos.

**Project: Design information technology solution to
change workflow for medical doctors
Reasons for failure:**

1. Organization did not define success, and there
   was no measurement for success.
2. Underestimated the work that needed to be
   done, resulting in a lack of resources or no
   staff assignment.
3. Sponsor did not want to hear bad news.
4. Organizational culture frowned on project delay
   and mistakes.

**Project: Simplify the process of receiving speci-
mens from nursing homes
Reasons for failure:**

1. The project's scope was too broad, and the
   leader/facilitator did not narrow the scope.
2. Staff were not included in the project design.
3. High staff turnover occurred during the project, suggesting a broader management problem; perhaps the employees did not feel valued
   as contributors.

■ What are the critical success factors in projects with long-
term sustainable gains?

Long-term sustainable gains are reached when the process becomes stable. With a stable process, further
improvements can be identified, and these improvements can be initiated.

In stable processes, it is easier to diagnose problems.

It is also important to truly understand the processes.
Complete a detailed work flow, current process map;
evaluate the process; and identify the areas to begin.

- What you would like to have done differently to make the project successful?
  Create an environment that welcomes bad news.
  Define success and what it looks like.
  Define the set of metrics to measure success.
  Resource the project adequately.
  Start by watching what people do and then redesign the process; identify key actors who will play a critical role in project success; finally, the project needs to have full support of leadership.

Conclusion

The mechanics of process improvement are relatively simple. W. Edwards Deming and other quality consultants advocated that the techniques and tools can be used by anyone in an organization regardless of their knowledge of statistics. Misuse of these tools and methods or the lack of support will certainly lead to project failure. But, when teams faithfully use these tools and have the support of stakeholders and management, projects still fail and backsliding occurs all too often. Our research with those directly involved with process improvement in healthcare bears this out, but it also illustrates that improvements built on unstable processes are likely to fail or the gains will not be sustained. Therefore, to have a successful project with lasting gains, the process that is improved must first be stable.

Chapter 4

Cleaning Up: Developing a Standardized, Optimized, Aligned Process

---

Introduction

As a manager or administrator, you know that good intentions, hard work, and creative solutions frequently end up amounting to less than what you expected. This is especially true in process improvement projects. Gains that you carefully estimate do not materialize, procedures that you dutifully fix backslide to their former state, and you are left with a dizzying array of confusion, missed opportunities, and workarounds until you abandon or kill the improvement project that you initiated in the hope of addressing some bit of entrenched dysfunction.

Then comes denial, delusion, and blame. You cannot believe your process improvement project was destined to join the 70% of all process improvement projects that fail.

In the project review, you question the support from leadership, departments, and staff or blame the inputs, environment, communication, people, and even the patient. Maybe there were unclear expectations or unprepared staff on the project team. Maybe not everyone embraced the goals or vision of the team or the mission of the project. You know that the process improvement techniques that you used, the improvement gurus that you follow, and the project management techniques and software that you were using have worked in the past. Yet, despite those past successes, your project failed or failed to meet your expectations. What happened?

Providing healthcare has become a complicated process. Especially in the United States, environmental complications arise from the payment structure, the regulations and review agencies, and even from the willingness of customers to conform to directions provided by caregivers. We would not associate process improvement failures directly to these issues. Based on our experience and research, failure to reach lasting process improvement originates in implementing changes to a process that is not stabilized, an issue that is not effectively addressed by process improvement techniques. Stabilization prior to improvement is frequently overlooked in many process improvement methodologies, especially in healthcare. In the manufacturing industry, improvements are built on standardized products and processes where there is minimal variation. This is not always the case in healthcare.

As we showed in the previous chapter, improvement efforts applied to an unstable, suboptimized, misaligned process can only result in missed opportunities and, ultimately, grand failure. True process improvement methodologies seek to fix broken processes, but lasting improvements can only occur when a process is already stable. It is like a doctor who gives a pain shot in the right knee of an injured, slightly overweight, high school football player. It solves the problem at hand quickly and efficiently but does not address the misaligned and damaged knee joint or take into account the effect of the player's weight. Ideally, the player would be carefully examined and his condition stabilized before any course of action is taken.

One of our friends is a highly sought-after auto mechanic who always has more business than time. When asked how he diagnoses a particularity difficult problem in a nonworking vehicle, his first step is always to clean away the grease and grime that builds up on a car. From there, he takes apart and cleans all of the potentially damaged parts, and when he is sure that the part is clean and working properly, he reassembles the parts and tests the car. From this point, he can diagnose the problem without all of the potential distractions from an unstable system of parts. It takes longer, he says, but a car is never returned because his "fix" failed, he never receives customer complaints, and the word-of-mouth advertising he receives keeps his business growing.

What he has learned is that repairing a car is only successful when the car is in a stable state. Similarly, process improvements can only succeed by starting from a stable state.

In healthcare, we have advocated this same concept. And, to help the administrators, directors, managers, supervisors, and staff remember this concept, we frequently remind them that you cannot improve what has not already gone through a good cleaning. You need a standardized, optimized, aligned process. You need SOAP (Figure 4.1).

Is Your Process Standardized, Optimized, and Aligned?

An organization such as a hospital is made up of a series of intertwined departments providing services for the benefit of customers. Within each department is a system that is dependent on the process that feeds its inputs and is simultaneously charged with providing the inputs needed for the next process. Yet, few managers understand the processes within their organization or how their department's processes are embedded in the goals of the organization. Administrators and managers focus on managing people, whom they profess to

Figure 4.1   Standardized, optimized, aligned process (SOAP).

understand, when they should be managing processes, which are notoriously more difficult to navigate. Sadly, every day's news brings stories of faulty and expensive products created by processes that are not stable, optimized, and aligned. In hospitals, the most dramatic evidence of this phenomenon is found in the 100,000 avoidable deaths caused by hospital medical errors each year in the United States, a figure roughly three times the number of people who die on our highways.[1]

Does your hospital focus on achieving organizational goals without being aware of how the underlying processes work? Is there an accurate picture of how the organization's processes are intertwined, codependent, interrelated, or even in conflict? Not understanding the processes that make up work functions and how the output of each department's functions becomes the input of the next department signals a misaligned system and ensures suboptimization within and between departments. Sustainable success requires understanding the processes that make your products for your customer. Everyone in the organization should intimately understand the processes they are responsible for and the process in the levels above and below them.

In fact, people should be working for the process, not the department they are assigned. The main process and the preliminary, parallel, and subsequent processes may be formed into departments for managerial reasons, but the focus of staff and management needs to be first on their process and how it fits into the entire system. The allegiance to departments and the silos they belong to inhibits discussion of the series of processes used to provide a product or service.

This point was driven home well into our careers in process improvement when our new chief financial officer (CFO), who had no experience in hospitals or healthcare (much to the chagrin of the entire finance group) and had come from a bank 2,000 miles away, asked us to prepare a flowchart of the entire hospital inpatient process, from preadmission to final billing. We explained that this was not possible. There were too many variations, twists, and turns that a patient can take when moving through a hospital stay. Each department did its autonomous part in providing care. He insisted. We thought that he clearly did not understand the impossibility of this request. He went on to explain that everything is a process, and that to understand how to improve the process, it needed to be documented.

We went back and considered the potential size of the paper that this would require; the sheer number of process boxes, decision diamonds, information flows; and the level of complexity of a *macro* process flow diagram like this. We were not even sure anyone could prepare something like this. With years of experience in hospitals and multitudes of healthcare degrees, we did not know all of the major operations. Looking back, for every $10 of savings, staff reductions, and process improvements that we had made, the hospital probably received $2. We did not fully understand all of the processes, and we knew that most of the department directors and administrators likely also did not (Figure 4.2).

Still, the CFO was insistent. We acquiesced but asked if we could start with a high-level macroflow diagram and move to increasingly detailed microflow diagrams. He agreed and indi-

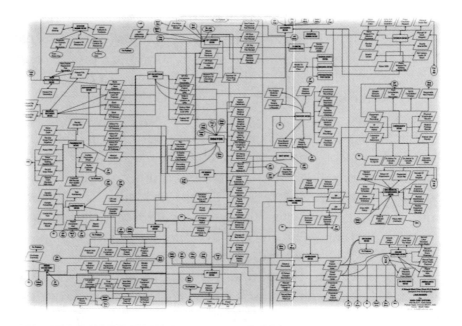

Figure 4.2   Example of a complex system.

cated that he expected the other administrators to prepare or request detailed flow diagrams for their own benefit.

The high-level macroflow diagram was enough to help him not only understand the hospital inpatient process but also see where his functions interacted with other functions in the hospital and how the processes he was in charge of fed or were fed by other functions. The original flowchart was complicated to the point that it did not help the CFO understand the operations. A simplified, high-level diagram was then developed and despite his limited healthcare experience, this diagram helped him to make better decisions (see Figure 4.3). To make decisions that were beneficial for all, however, he needed a more complete understanding of the entire hospital process and the macro-level interactions between them.

The patient-centered care diagram was helpful, but as a CFO more information on the direct interactions and the magnitude of each operation was needed to support

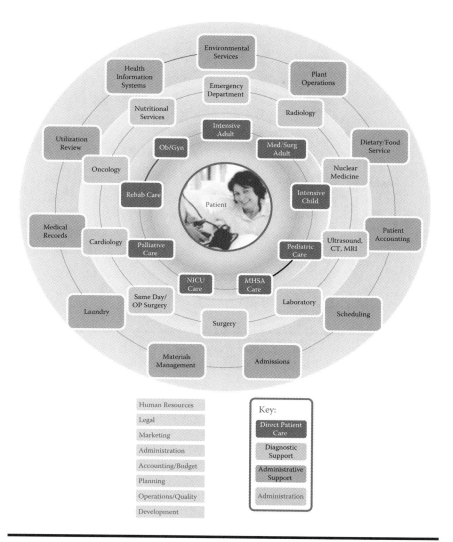

Figure 4.3   The patient-care-centered hospital.

decision making. Organization charts showed who reported to whom but did not explain how services and processes interacted. The flowchart of all interactions in the hospital was much too detailed to follow much less use to make decisions. The CFO needed to understand the functions that made up the care delivery system at the 10,000-foot level and then dive into specific functions to understand how

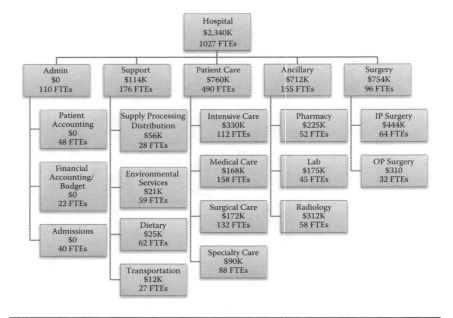

Figure 4.4   High-level functional tree structure. FTE = full-time equivalent; IP = inpatient; OP = outpatient.

they worked. Organization charts and detailed flow charts did not provide the information needed to manage change. Thus began the birth of functional tree structures (FTSs) (Figure 4.4).

Standard in almost every organization is some type of performance appraisal process and output monitoring system. These measurement tools often govern how people manage their processes. These tools also affect operations. People will strive to meet their stated objectives even if they do not fit in with the goals of their department, adjacent departments, or customer expectations. To complicate the issue, if anyone in the chain from manager to frontline producer has an incomplete or inaccurate understanding of the system they are associated with or if there are misaligned goals, environmental constraints, inefficient work procedures, and faulty communications, problems will arise. Any of these problems can instantly suboptimize an entire unit and sometimes the business units around it. A solid understanding of the functions and interactions within an organization, ensuring that these functions produce what customers expect and aligning the goals of the appraisal and monitoring systems, creates a highly effective organization. The FTS simplifies and makes visible the practice of understanding, optimizing, and aligning processes so that they produce services that meet customers' expectations. FTS is both a top-down and bottom-up process that helps to create a stable system.

Creating the FTS diagrams from the top organizational level down to the individual processes will immediately help to identify issues, but before process improvement projects begin, all processes must be stabilized. Fortunately, the process of stabilization will lead to improvements in quality and reductions in cost.

Soap: Standardized

Most healthcare managers and workers are just trying to keep up with workloads. It is rare that they have the time to think about possible opportunities for improvement and optimization of their activities and efforts. When they have worked on department or multidepartment improvements, the efforts are initially successful, but after the focus on the new processes wanes and the additional support of internal or external consults has ended, the departments slide back to the old mode of operation, and all the gains wither on the vine. Hastily built on unstable processes, short-term gains fade all too quickly; the gains erode as operations return to their initial unstable state. This is frequently referred to as "backsliding." In the book *Who Killed Change*, authors Ken Blanchard, John Britt, Pat Zigarmi, and Judd Hoekstra cited: "Every day organizations around the world launch change initiatives—often big, expensive ones—designed to improve the status quo. Yet 50 to 70 percent of these change efforts fail.[2]"

There is no reason to believe that this rate of backsliding with healthcare process improvement does not occur, and in fact, we believe it to be worse. Certainly, the complexity of providing care makes healthcare a difficult industry in which to create lasting improvements. Yet, today's focus on the cost and outcomes in the United States makes improvement a necessity. If 70% or more of operational and quality improvement projects fail to show gains or improvements after nine months, then we have wasted all of the effort made and money spent on improvements. How then, do we create lasting change?

The question looms large in every manager's mind, but the answer is deceptively simple. It turns out that the 70% of process improvement projects that fail to meet their expected objectives were built on the equivalent of shifting sands, while the successful 30% of projects were built on a well-understood and relatively stable structure. The first and most important task to accomplish before any process improvement venture is to make sure that there is a stable structure to build on. That cannot be done without clearly understanding what the process is supposed to produce, what the contribution of each process is to the entire organizational objective (i.e., taking care of inpatients), whether the process is currently optimized, and finally having a clear understanding of each step in the process.

The building blocks of most of the standard process improvement methods, such as the Shewhart Plan-Do-Check ("Study")-Act cycle, consist of identifying issues, searching for root causes, developing solutions to those root causes, and implementing solutions. Regardless of the process improvement methodology, we have found that a project's success is predicated entirely on the stability of the underlying structure it is designed to improve. The complexity and uncertainty that often surround processes that are in need of improvement are often the primary cause of process improvement failures.

Guidepost 1: Long-term project sustainability only occurs when process improvement is built on a stable process.

sOap: Optimized

Imagine a car owner whose front passenger tire keeps going flat. At the tire store, he asks the technician for a tire that cannot go flat. The technician, without bothering to inquire about the size of the other tires, provides a tire that is resistant to punctures but is slightly larger than the other tires. For the first week, the driver is happy that the tire does not go flat, but the lopsided car now pulls to the right; after a few near mishaps as the car drifts between lanes, the driver decides to go back and obtain a tire the same size as the original. The car now tracks straight but continues to go flat.

The technician solved the problem of tires going flat, but the lack of understanding of the entire operational needs of the driver caused a steering problem. Cars optimally run with same-size, puncture-resistant tires that are inflated to the correct pressure. While quickly solving the car owner's problem, the technician overlooked the entire essence of driving a car. Similarly, many people join the quality improvement bandwagon hoping to make a difference for the customers they serve but become frustrated as solutions do not pan out and customers are unappreciative. Listening to customers and providing what they want does not cut it. Understanding the entire set of requirements, those spoken and those adjacent to the current process, is the only way to provide effective solutions.

This same situation occurs in healthcare. Emergency room (ER) staff wishing to improve the "door-to-doc" time (the time between when a patient enters the front door of an ER to the time the patient is first seen by a doctor) can achieve the shortest time by moving the registration process to discharge. Is this innovative? Yes? Will it save time and expense while continuing to collect the required billing information? Let us see.

It is not until we look at the entire process—all of the steps or processes that need to occur during an ER visit—that we can tell whether moving the registration process to discharge is optimal. The Emergency Department (ED) does not operate in a vacuum. Other departments will need information that originates from the ED. The ED must synchronize with radiology, laboratory, and pharmacy processes and the activities of other support departments. Changes made in a vacuum tend to lead to suboptimized solutions. The ED's decision to register patients during discharge makes sense to the ED, but the doctor may want to see previous x-rays and laboratory tests that the patient may have at the hospital, requiring a patient identification number to look this up. The additional speed observed by the ED will most certainly cause disruptions in services to the physician, ancillary departments, and other areas. In other words, the sustainability of the improvement in the ER cannot and will not last if not coordinated—optimized—with all other processes upstream from, concurrent with, and downstream from the ED.

Another example we encountered occurred when the operating room (OR) started scheduling two back-to-back orthopedic cases in the same operating suite. Because they were going to use the same staff, the staff was asked to help with the room turnaround process. They successfully reduced room turnaround time to less than 15 minutes, but they had not synchronized the activities between the OR and central sterile supply and preop. Back-to-back orthopedic surgeries required the same expensive set of instruments, and the cleaning of these instruments could not be done within 15 minutes. Therefore, the next case was always delayed, showing that when physicians, nurses, and other staff focus on only their part of the process, without synchronizing their actions with the entire process, solutions do not provide optimal benefits. Sometimes, it turns into a conflict of interest between process improvement teams within a department rather the cooperation needed to address issues.

Guidepost 2: Optimization reduces waste in materials, time, and talent. Improvements built on processes that are not optimized add to the waste.

---

soAp: Aligned

One department's success can translate into three departments' failures. In manufacturing, if the goal of production is to build 1,000 parts each day, of the warehouse is to safely hold every part until it is sold to a customer, and of sales to sell 1,000 units per day, it would appear that the three goals are aligned. But, if sales on average are 900 units per day, production still makes 1,000 units a day, and the warehouse can only hold 2,000 parts, the warehouse will run out of room in roughly 20 days. Pallets will be stacked, spoiled parts increase, and overall efficiency declines. Those in production are praised, in sales are shamed, and in the warehouse are reprimanded for their losses. Problems arise between the people in production, warehouse, and sales. Sales begins monitoring each individual's sales performance, and team collaboration declines. For fear of missing their goal, production will not want to reduce its output, and the warehouse will stack extra parts in hallways and on top of other parts. Oddly, in this scenario, production, warehouse, and sales will do their best to meet their goal despite how it affects the other business units. Profitability and employee engagement will suffer, and customer satisfaction will decline as sales presses hard to sell more to current clients and spoiled units are sent to customers.

This illustration is a simplification of a production facility, but it also mirrors the typical day at a hospital. The ED builds its budgets on 50,000 visits and 25,000 admissions per year, a modest 2% decrease over the past year. The ancillary departments all budget for this decrease accordingly. The support departments like food service and environmental services work toward balancing staff and preparing for the decrease. The "sales" department here is the community and doctors who send their patients to the ER. But, what if one of the local urgent care clinics closes? Patients who once went to the urgent care clinic may divert to the hospital. Can the emergency, ancillary, and support departments be flexible with their staffing and supply purchases to compensate for the slight increase in demand? Will the ancillary departments be held to their staffing and supply budgets based on lower volumes? If the demand increases and the ER does everything in its power to handle this increase yet the support departments cannot provide for adequate throughput, who will be at fault?

This problem with goals and staffing is only one way that processes become misaligned. The products of one department or function within the department can be optimized for that department but misaligned with the department receiving the first department's output. To become more customer focused, one hospital allowed each outpatient ancillary department to schedule its own patients. Not only did this turn out to be more costly, but also it turned into a nightmare for patients who wanted to schedule more than one appointment with doctors and ancillary departments. The separate scheduling functions created yet another problem when each department and physician's office provided inconsistent and nonstandardized data, which the outpatient coders need to use for billing. Alignment is a two-dimensional concept. Departments need to consider alignment both "within" (internal to the department) and "between" departments. The tools and processes used to ensure alignment use different Lean tools to address capacity while creating a specific set of product/service specifications to ensure high-quality services, eliminating errors and minimizing waste.

For any operational improvement initiative to succeed, all of the processes *and* parties involved (doctors, nurses, clinical and support staff, etc.) must be stable, optimized, and aligned. Even if the entire staff is incentivized to participate in the process improvement, sustainability will be a challenge. Therefore, at the beginning of each operational improvement journey, it is imperative to clearly define and communicate the roles and responsibilities of everyone directly and indirectly involved with the process. The following factors will cause rapid breakdown of recently improved processes, relegating them to the 70% dustbin:

- Lack of defined and documented processes and standard of work
- Lack of defined roles and responsibilities for all parties involved
- Little or no training
- Missing or nonexistent training materials
- Missing or nonexistent reference materials
- Lack of SMART (simple, measurable, accurate and actionable, reliable and relevant, timely) metrics

As part of the organization's leadership, it is absolutely essential that you define and communicate your role and responsibilities to your staff. You must understand each one of your hospital's processes almost as intimately as the staff on the ground. Remember that management supports production; it is not production's responsibility to support management. Management's understanding and, more important, support of production lead to efficiency and overall effectiveness. It is the classic "inverted" managerial hierarchy that supports sustained process improvements.

Guidepost 3: Goals and objectives that are not aligned within and between functions promote anarchy in operations.

To summarize the importance of having a standardized, optimized, and aligned process, let us look at the outcomes from each of the possible scenarios (Table 4.1).

Summing It All Up

Decisions and actions based on erroneous assumptions create inefficiencies, waste, and possibly danger. This is especially true in processes that are operating in an unstable environment, and the consequences in a healthcare setting can be dire. For example, everyone accepts that a registered nurse (RN) owns a specific set of skills and knowledge. An RN working within his or her function, fully aware of the roles and responsibilities and standard of work of his or her functional unit, provides the expected and, it is hoped, high-quality outcome. Frequently, a nursing department must rely on staffing that comes from an outside nurse staffing agency, whose nurses also have a specific set of skills and knowledge. An agency RN therefore should function competently if aware of the specific work flow and standardized processes at the hospital where he or she has been assigned. But, if the agency nurse has not been briefed about the hospital's processes and does not have easy access to the training and reference materials for the unit the nurse will be working in, there is great possibility that the agency RN may endanger the well-being of the patients and expose the institution to litigation. In addition, this lack of understanding of the processes will create bottlenecks to the operations, hindering other nurses' performance. This would never be the intention of the agency RN; it is just

Table 4.1   Predicted Outcomes of SOAP

Standardized Everyone does it the same way	Optimized Everyone does it in the same order	Aligned Inputs meet my needs and outputs meet the customer's needs	Outcome
Yes	Yes	No	Highly consistent output that will not meet the customer's needs
Yes	No	Yes	Costly and potentially untimely product
No	Yes	Yes	Inconsistent output that infrequently meets customer specifications
No	No	Yes	Costly, dangerous, and potentially untimely product
Yes	No	No	Organized chaos
No	Yes	No	Dangerous product that will not meet the customer's needs
No	No	No	Low quality, high costs, poor outcomes, dangerous situation (this is more prevalent then you'd like to know)
Yes	Yes	Yes	A product that is stable, uniform, and meets the customer's needs

that skills and knowledge are not enough for the agency RN to provide a safe, effective, and efficient product and service.

Endnotes

1. Kohn, L. T., Corrigan, J., & Donaldson, M. S. (2000). *To Err Is Human: Building a Safer Health System*. Washington, DC: National Academy Press.
2. Source: Blanchard, K., Britt, J., Zigarmi, P., and Hoekstra, J. (2009). *Who Killed Change? Solving the Mystery of Leading People through Change*. New York: Morrow. http://www.kenblanchard.com/whokilledchange/.

Chapter 5

Know Your Processes

In the previous chapters, we noted that half of the healthcare process improvement projects we surveyed failed to meet their objectives and maintain gains. Despite the reasons managers gave for poor project results, creating change in an environment that is not prepared for change is the ultimate culprit. We are not talking about the softer skills, such as organizational readiness and acceptance of change management principles and techniques. We contend that making changes to an ever-changing and poorly understood combination of dynamic processes can only result in failure.

We start with the simple concept of the input/process/output diagram frequently used to describe a system. Improving a process requires inputs that respond to the voice of the process, outputs that respond to the customer expectations heard in the voice of the customer, and a stable process that can consistently convert the inputs into the expected outputs. This appears simple (Figure 5.1).

But, healthcare, like many service industries, is a combination of complex and dynamic systems.[1]

A *complex system* is a composition of sophisticated parts, such as electronic funds transfer in the banking system or a fighter jet. For example, if each part of a fighter jet is built to

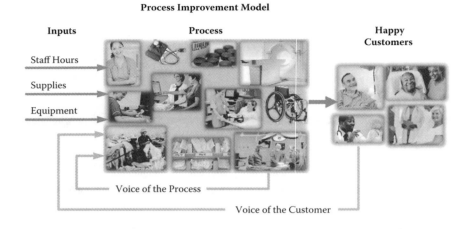

Figure 5.1   The simple process improvement model.

complete specifications, assembled as defined in the blue-prints, and maintained as identified in the maintenance documents, the system will function as expected. Likewise, if the electronic transactions within the banking system follow expected protocols and the system is carefully built and orchestrated to debit and credit the correct accounts, everything functions as expected. The specifications and maintenance of complicated systems are carefully executed because anything less could cause catastrophic consequences and be financially disastrous. Not all complex systems are as technically intricate as a fighter jet. The inpatient elective admission process can be a complex system consisting of highly scripted interactions between procedures and information systems. But, once variations in human inputs and processes come into play—and, with them, judgment and interpretation—the system transforms from a complex system into a dynamic system.

A *dynamic system* can consist of not only complex systems but also a unique set of attributes that can change. These attributes can appear random, uncontrollable, and manual. Almost all systems involving people or decisions are dynamic systems. The simplest example of a dynamic system can be seen in a set of twins. Despite having the same genes from the same parents and living in the same environment with the same inputs, the twins frequently respond differently to stimuli. One twin will like dance and the other soccer, one will not eat bananas and the other will not eat raisins. Although they may be similar in many respects, their actions are not predictable. Numerous twin studies have demonstrated that the responses two people make to the same stimuli are not the same.

So, also, can similarly situated patients within the same hospital have different experiences. Two male patients receiving a standard computed tomographic (CT) scan receive two different sets of services. Why? Their body structures, their temperament, their ability to be still, even their body fat make them different. The technician doing the test, the time the transporter brought the patient in, the skill of the technician, and the process followed can vary with each patient. Many complicated systems consist of a large number of human and complex system interactions that function in an environment where human interactions, human psychology, and history all have an effect on the process inputs. This does not even take into account the possible emotional responses.

Creating lasting changes in complex systems is infinitely easier compared to dynamic systems. A production line at the jet factory, where all of the inputs to each station are highly standardized and the process performed is highly controlled, creates a known outcome. The blueprints and design documents describe in detail the materials, sizes, assembly, and entire functionality. If there are no changes to the materials used or the timing of their arrival in the process, then you have a stable process. If the output needs to be improved, perhaps to increase the wingspan or apply a new type of radar-absorbing stealth coating, changes start in a stable environment. Outcomes can be reliably measured, and the changes to the materials or processes will result in an improved product.

Dynamic systems require an additional step. With inputs likely to have substantial variations and processes that are not highly standardized, the outputs have a greater likelihood of changing. Therefore, these variations in the inputs and processes need to be taken into account. Better yet, any standardization of the characteristics of a dynamic system will make it easier to make changes with a high probability of lasting success. With this in mind, we can evaluate the success and failure of healthcare projects and, over time, the sustainability of improvement efforts.

To understand why healthcare is more than a complex system, let us review the history of healthcare and the economic incentives that have governed the provision of health services for the past 50 years. Almost immediately after the passage of the Medicare and Medicaid programs in the mid-1960s, the rate of utilization in healthcare began to increase because care was now paid for by someone other than the person who received the care. Hospitals and doctors quickly realized they were paid for what they did and not for the outcomes. The indemnity, point-of-service (POS), preferred provider organization (PPO), and health maintenance organization (HMO) plans along with providers (hospitals and physicians) paid for and ordered procedures that may not have been needed. Whether it was considered "defensive medicine" or just economic survival, providers were encouraged to provide as many services as possible. Although the purpose of Medicare and Medicaid and commercial insurance was to create better access to healthcare, it has in effect increased unnecessary utilization and costs while increasing the opportunity for error.

Some changes in healthcare reimbursement sought to reduce unnecessary utilization and reward better clinical outcomes. Although the implementation of payments based on diagnosis-related groups (DRGs) and relative value units (RVUs) in the 1980s initially helped decrease the rapid growth in healthcare cost, the growth in healthcare cost superseded the U.S. Consumer Price Index in all but a brief time in the 1990s. DRGs and RVUs were introduced as tools that would reduce unnecessary care. Another aim was to create an environment in which the services rendered would become the same across providers and patients. Still, we continue to see a high degree of variation in the services provided and cost between providers, institutions, regions, and states for the same DRG. This variation continues to frustrate health policy analysts, but it can be easily explained in the intricacy of human responses to improving one's economic well-being, social orders, and governmental regulations. Everyone within the entire process is working toward their own economic best interest.

The cadres of consultants and experts brought in to solve these hospital-specific problems seldom reduced costs and improved quality at the facility for any reasonable period of time. After three months, the savings began to evaporate. While the consultants observed and questioned employees, collected reams of data, produced a bound report, and made great promises of improvement, observable and measurable improvements began to erode as process variation and input variation crept back into the dynamic system.

There are many possible reasons for the lack of continued success but our experience and research suggest that this "backsliding" comes from implementing changes in a vacuum where most processes are not standardized, optimized, and aligned. The poor outcomes are frequently blamed on four issues:

- Lack of understanding of the entire set of processes and systems at work
- Lack of appropriate skills by process owners and process improvement teams before, during, and after the project
- Lack of relevancy of the recommendations to the department operations
- Lack of support by internal staff, external customers, management, or suppliers

Was it that the techniques were flawed? Were the great improvements seen in manufacturing, first in Germany and Japan and later in the United States, relevant only to manufacturing and irrelevant to service organizations—especially dynamic organizations like hospitals? Both manufacturing and service organizations are complex in nature, but the communication between staff in manufacturing is straighter and roles and responsibilities are more defined in manufacturing. The nature of the processes requires that manufacturing organizations establish a standardized and aligned set of processes that eliminate the dynamic aspects.

In the early 1980s, Ford Motor reintroduced Dr. W. Edwards Deming to America. Although Deming had tried to convince American manufacturers to use his methods in the 1950s, he was unable to persuade them and turned to more welcoming ears in Japan, which was rebuilding its manufacturing processes after World War II. Since the 1960s, competition from foreign car companies had steadily eroded Ford's market share and profitability. Starved for methods to catch up to the quality levels of Toyota and Honda, Ford invited Deming to teach the company his Continuous Quality Improvement (CQI) methods for manufacturing. Eventually, these methods helped the company improve quality and regain market acceptance as a provider of higher-quality vehicles. All of the American automobile manufacturers went to see firsthand what the Japanese and European manufacturers were doing.

During this same period, healthcare institutions, responding to the pressures of insurance payers, began adopting quality improvement techniques and integrating Deming's methods in healthcare. Their success was sporadic, and improvements frequently were short lived. Some organizations dropped or reduced their support for CQI and similar programs. Even though they worked in Japan and in manufacturing, the CQI process had limited success in American hospitals, where cultural differences and a short-term focus on solutions and return on investment (ROI) seemed to keep process improvement from being successful. Some of the basic quality steps were not fully understood, processes were poorly documented, and standardization was never achieved. Project management tools were introduced with limited success. And,

Figure 5.2   Outcomes of a misunderstood department.

even if they were successful in the near term, these tools do
not guarantee the sustainability of the operational or quality improvements. Are cultural and operational differences
the barrier to sustainability and success of healthcare process
improvement projects, or is healthcare an amalgamation of
dynamic systems that needs to be simplified (Figure 5.2)?

There are many possible factors, but our hypothesis was
that the primary reason that projects failed was that there
was not a shared understanding of the current structure of
the department and how the department's functions fit within
all of the other functions in the hospital. This is further com-
pounded by misalignment of goals and incentives, unclear
project scope, lack of skills or training, and an unstable environment within the hospital.

Hospitals, like many organizations, revert to operating
within a "silo" structure in which communication and knowledge are shared up and down the silo but not across silos.
Most patient functions involve crossing multiple silos each
day. The people working in each silo have limited knowledge

of the functional requirements across silos, even those they interact with daily. Unfortunately, many people in charge of managing these functions also do not know the functional requirements across silos. Therefore, they are unaware or lack knowledge of

- Interdepartmental processes
- Intradepartmental functions, processes, and critical input variables by each process
- Communication between and within departments and functions within a department
- Product/service specifications and requirements
- Cross-training of required skills
- Ongoing staff training

This lack of knowledge is further complicated by institutional problems such as

- Structural instability (including functions and processes)
- Poor knowledge of the entire system
- Performance incentives that are in conflict with the incentives of other departments, providers, and hospitals within a system
- The competitive environment created between departments
- Mistrust between department staff and leadership

Without a clear understanding of the relationships between processes, service and quality decline. Few healthcare staff can describe how their roles and responsibilities relate to subsequent processes, especially if those processes are outside their department. This condition keeps hospitals from being effective, leads to errors, and inhibits possible quality and productivity enhancements.

The complexity of many healthcare organizations drives staff to be locally focused instead of having a broader worldview. This mindset can be changed when staff

- Work within a stable process
- Understand not only their process but also all preceding and following processes
- Understand how their function fits into the bigger picture within their function, within their department, within their division, within the entire organization, compared to other organizations' products and services and, most important, within the minds of the final consumer

To understand why many process improvement projects fail to create lasting improvements, we spent a decade working with teams, creating and testing theories and looking for ways to support process improvement teams. We believed that CQI is valuable and that it could work not only in 1950s Japanese car manufacturing but also in 1990s American healthcare. Through interactions with all levels of healthcare leaders and reviewing projects that failed to meet their projected goals, it became evident that the dynamism of the healthcare system made it difficult to build lasting improvements. The underlying structure, interactions, and information flow, together with numerous and varied players, made a system that was constantly and dynamically changing. The structural environment and economic incentives were different for everyone involved.

Maybe creating healthcare flow charts is too complicated. Maybe it is not an industry that can be improved with techniques and tools effective in the production line world. But, we began to ask, what, really, is the difference between manufacturing and healthcare? Certainly, building cars is a complex process. Could healthcare be transformed from being dynamic to being just complex? We soon found the answer by focusing on structure. In successful process improvement projects, like those at Toyota, every worker shares a strong and complete understanding of their processes, their structure, and the relationship between their processes and all processes before and after them. Based on this common and shared knowledge, each worker not only owns their process but also employs their best efforts to improve, adjust, or redesign the process so that it fits more efficiently into the entire process. The continuity of understanding the chain of processes and the focus on standardization first, and only then improvement, creates the opportunity for sustainability of new improvements.

This focus on structure also plays a significant role in thwarting suboptimization and misalignment. Newly proposed improvements thrive within well-structured, stable, and normalized environments. As with manufacturing's production line, structure provides the foundation for understanding the current process, identifying opportunities to improve, and synchronizing changes and new processes.

Without a stable and well-defined functional structure, your organization's growth and progress are doomed. We realized that administrators, department directors, and even employees often could not visualize or completely describe all of the functions, products, or services that their own department offered. Therefore, the first step toward creating lasting improvements was to gain an understanding of the structure and systems—both complex (just the machine) and dynamic (machine plus human)—within your organization. Everyone in your hospital should also know exactly how their unit fits into the larger organizational picture: what units it collaborates (and sometimes competes) with, where in the process their work comes in, and what role they play in the organization's mission. To give managers an intuitive, visual tool to accomplish this seemingly impossible task, we developed the functional tree structure (FTS).

The FTS starts with a pictorial representation that systematically maps, in increasing detail, the full range of main, secondary, and tertiary functions, activities, and tasks used to understand the structure and function of the department. The only way to effectively achieve organizational and departmental goals—well, the only way to *develop* plausible organizational and department goals—is to understand the structure. Likewise, to improve a process, departments need to fully understand the functions and structure of their part of the organization and how they fit within prior and subsequent functions.

The FTS provides a profound understanding of functions within the interrelated, dynamic environment where they continuously operate. The FTS allows you to map the functions, subfunctions, processes, and subprocesses of an operation and conduct a statistical analysis of the outcomes of the process. When we get to this level of detail and look at the outcomes of processes—especially in healthcare—what becomes painfully evident is the amount of variation in the outcomes. The outcomes of one process become the input to the next process. This variation causes numerous problems for processes downstream of our process.

Becoming Six Sigma compliant, which involves looking for less than 1 defect in 294,117 operations, becomes impossible in healthcare largely because of the variation in healthcare processes. But, that is OK. Knowing that there is inherent variation in the process forces us to learn more about the process, each input variable, and the staff and mechanical interactions in the process, so that we can manage process variation and, over time, decrease that variation. Sustainable or breakthrough improvements come when they are built on a stable structure—one with minimal variation. But, striving to achieve *true* Six Sigma quality is a waste of effort. That is not to say that the Six Sigma process should not be used; it is just that it is more relevant in healthcare to strive for a Five Sigma quality level for which 999 of 1,000 processes achieve satisfactory outcome specifications. Someday, true Six Sigma quality *can* be the goal.

The FTS helps departments visualize the nuts and bolts of what actually takes place. It provides the details of the operations of departments, increases staff buy-in for the importance of every role, and becomes an effective tool for communicating the focus and function of every department. It simplifies process understanding for leaders and helps each department set reasonable objectives and goals. It visually explains the purpose of the department easily and objectively by documenting the what, why, when, where, who, how, and how often.

Using the FTS, staff can state their role and responsibility and can connect their daily activities to the larger scope of the department's and organization's objectives. Every department will

- Know who their customers and suppliers are
- Learn the service specifications their customers need
- Know why and how their products/services are used
- Learn their customers' demand patterns
- Learn how to adjust their product delivery rate
- Develop detailed guidelines for acceptance or refusal of any inputs that they receive

Most important, implementing the FTSs provides a robust starting structure for process improvement, Lean, and Six Sigma initiatives. It supports the pride of workmanship, eliminates waste and duplication of effort, and helps organizations become "best in class." Process improvement projects flourish under the stable structure that the FTS provides. Gains are greater and sustained. Improvements can be seen in one or more of the following best-in-class metrics:

- Best-in-class cost: The cost of production or service delivery, including all fixed and variable costs, is lower than those of competitors. The services do not have to be the same and can be complementary or substitute services, but the cost to provide the services and the price customers pay have to be less than those of competitors or alternatives. Being best in class with regard to cost means higher profitability.
- Best-in-class quality: Seen from either the customer's point of view or in a reduction in errors, litigation, and rework, organizational improvements that lead to products or

services that are demonstrated better than those of competitors means that there will be a shift in demand to the best-in-class quality provider. Being best in class with regard to quality means preferred pricing.

■ Best-in-class service: Whether the service measures are on-time delivery or customer satisfaction with staff interactions, hospitals are rated and compared based on the service they provide. Word of mouth and national rating agencies provide consumers information on the level of service for each health institution. Being best in class with regard to service ensures repeat business.

Few organizations achieve the trifecta of being best in all three, and they do not need to achieve it. Being best in two ensures growth, being best in one ensures survival. Being best in none ensures demise. We believe that every organization should strive to be best in class in at least one, if not all three, of these best-in-class criteria. Long term, organizations that are not best in class in at least one criterion will go out of business.

There are viable examples of healthcare organizations that have reached best-in-class distinctions in at least two of these three criteria. Recently, hospitals like Virginia Mason and Geisinger showed measurable results from their focus and effort toward becoming best in class. Renowned institutions such as the Cleveland Clinic, the Mayo Clinic, M. D. Anderson, and others are also seen as having best-in-class quality or service. A number of hospitals have focused on best-in-class costs and have financial stability coveted by organizations whose costs are higher. To become a renowned and respected organization requires discipline. Not everyone plays golf like Tiger Woods, basketball like Michael Jordan, or tennis like Serena Williams. Their greatness came from focused effort, great discipline, and the right genes. But, organizations can certainly improve their products and services to become best-in-class players with that same focused effort and discipline. And, it all starts with standardization and uniformity of processes and that takes great effort and discipline.

One feature commonly observed in best-in-class organizations is a strong understanding of structure that spans across all employees. In one form or another, they have perfected something similar to the FTS approach—either directly or intuitively. Best-in-class organizations do not need to prepare for the Joint Commission (formerly the Joint Commission on Accreditation for Healthcare Organizations; JCAHO), health plan, or Centers for Medicare and Medicaid Services (CMS) audits. These healthcare organizations are ready for any review 24/7.

The FTS should be used at all levels within an organization, providing a reliable map of the organization for every manager and staff member to guide both daily processes and future change. Based on our experiences, we fully expect that most readers are saying: "But, I already understand how my function fits into the organization and how my outputs support the subsequent process." We have heard this type of statement at all levels of an organization. Worse yet, we have heard managers say that they do not need to know the details and expect their people to handle the nits—the small details associated with their jobs. If only either statement were true. Reviewing the components of the FTS always brings up unknown requirements, unexpected variations, misalignments, redundancies, and mysteries.

Most process improvement projects are built on top of this unknown, unstable, and highly variable process. It is similar to building a house on a major fault line, over a sinkhole, out of materials whose properties change at a moment's notice. Anything but good is likely to happen. Any improvements made are quickly erased.

With a clear understanding of the current structure, organizations can create transition plans. Improvements made on a stable structure last. Savings continue to come. Service does not slip. By first employing the FTS, process improvement processes like Lean and Six Sigma succeed. The purpose of the FTS is to facilitate organizations' transition to becoming best in class. The FTS provides the stable base that supports the transition and sets the stage for lasting improvements. The FTS begins the journey toward breakthrough improvements.

Endnote

1. This concept is further discussed in *Complicated and Complex Systems: What Would Successful Reform of Medicare Look Like?* (Glouberman, Sholom, and Zimmerman, Brenda. Commission on the Future of Health Care in Canada Discussion Paper No. 8. Ottawa: Commission on the Future of Health Care in Canada, July 2002).

Chapter 6

Functional Tree Structures

Introduction

The previous chapters focused on process: If the process is not "known," it cannot be stable or optimized. The goal of functional tree structures (FTSs) is first to understand or know the process at the microlevel and make sure that everyone is invested in the standardization, optimization, and alignment of their process with adjacent processes.

Most people rightfully say that they know what they are doing at work. But, for every time we have heard someone say they know what they are doing, we have also heard them say: "Where did the day go?" When we feel that the day rushed by—without achieving everything we had planned to do—it is likely that the "process" did not follow a standard course. Something occurred during the day that altered the process. Unexpected interruptions, unexpected work tasks, rework, inefficiencies, delays, mistakes, and a host of other issues have not only reduced our output but also likely reduced the quality of our output. Traditionally, process improvement teams have looked at this jumbled assortment of poorly documented tasks and tried to fix the rework, inefficiencies, delays, mistakes, and so on. During this exercise, the process may become more apparent to those on the team, but seldom does it become completely transparent. "Fixes" and well-intentioned improvements to this unstable process unravel quickly. It is the story we heard repeatedly when we interviewed process improvement team leaders about their successful and unsuccessful improvement projects. The process and all of its intricacies, inconsistencies, and idiosyncrasies was not known by the team. Not everyone in the department followed the same process every time.

Worse yet is when supervisors, managers, directors, and administrators set up methods to improve on the inefficiencies or reduce mistakes and institute unneeded steps in an already undocumented process. Every honest manager will admit that at some time in their career they established an edict or change to a process that did not improve the process. Every employee can recall when their manager instituted a bone-headed edict or change that did not help to improve or even monitor the process. It comes down to whether anyone truly understands the process.

We are not expecting that a senior manager or administrator understand all of the steps in performing a computed tomographic (CT) scan, but we are also adamant that a senior manager or administrator should never think of changing the process the CT scan team uses. The level of understanding of the process becomes higher the closer to the process that we are. The CT scan tech needs to know and understand the process from when the patient enters the room to when the patient exits the room. The scheduler and clerks do not need to know this, but they do need to know the scheduling processes and any information that the tech needs to have to accurately conduct the CT scan. The supervisor needs to know these procedures to train and monitor (with help and participation of other engaged team members) whether the procedures are accomplished correctly. The manager needs to know that scheduling needs to occur before the procedure. The manager, senior manager, or administrator facilitates improvements and supports the CT department and, despite wanting to implement improvements, should instead leave that to those involved and responsible for the process.

Remember, processes that are not stabilized and optimized will not produce the highest possible quality. The goal of the FTS is first to create a stable environment to build on before you eliminate non-value-added (unneeded) tasks and optimize operations. Our experience suggests that this structured approach is the best way to provide lasting quality improvements. The best and most current example of this is the number of checklists that have been recently developed for physicians in their treatment of specific diseases and conditions. The checklists have been credited with improving outcomes, improving care, reducing unnecessary tests and procedures, reducing costs, and freeing doctors to spend more time with patients. Essentially what physicians are doing is reducing variation in their practice, following a unified process, and using best practices. They have stabilized and optimized their process and improved the quality and outcomes of care, often by just implementing simple checklists. Using checklists and understanding the process are not dumbing down the way things are done. Rather, they improve the consistency and quality produced.

To begin our discussion of how the FTS supports quality, we need to define *quality* as consistent conformance to standards. Conformance to standards is when the actual outcome matches the desired outcome. For example, let us say that we define a quality outcome for the process between distribution and the operating rooms (ORs) as providing the instruments and supplies required for each operation on time so that there are zero delays in the OR. In this example, the quality is measured by the number of delays caused by missing instruments or supplies.

There may be additional standards required of this process. A quality outcome of surgery is not having infections caused by unclean instruments or supplies from distribution. A hospital that starts all surgeries on time but has 5% surgical infections caused by careless processes in distribution is not providing quality in the eyes of the end user. Therefore, quality or conformance to standards requires that we consider all of the possible customer expectations. Quality outcomes require

- A thorough understanding of what the customer (the patient, the doctor, the nurse, etc.) needs;
- Carefully described characteristics or measures of quality outcomes required to meet the customers' needs; and
- A stable operating platform to provide quality results consistently.

The first two requirements are presented in many books, so defining them again should not be necessary. The third requirement is our focus.

Quality results through conformance to a standard can only be obtained *and* maintained when there is a stable process that uses a proven method. In healthcare, the proven methods are generally called "evidenced-based" practices. Evidence-based practices are often inferred through reviewing clinical outcomes and associating them to the processes that supported the outcome. From a process engineering prospective, we want proof that the practices created the desired outcome. The process ultimately is producing better results, but which tasks within the process are creating these outcomes? Positive outcomes could occur strictly by chance. We would advocate that the processes be reviewed and standardized to reduce the opportunity for failure. Black box procedures may deliver desired results, but unless we understand why they deliver these results, anything good or bad can happen.

Automobile manufacturers will use a proven method or assembly for years to ensure that their products conform to standards. It does not make them innovative, but it does make them reliable, and reliability is a measurable outcome that conforms to customers' standards. If you look closely at any vehicle, although the exterior may look new, the windshield motors, seat tracks, alternator, compressor, door latches, and hundreds of other parts are reused every model year and on many vehicles. Here, quality is achieved by perfecting the process or inputs and using it as frequently as possible. One constant lesson learned from automotive manufacturers is that every part description, manufacturing process, and assembly process is carefully detailed and presented to the team of people making this component. Conformance to standard ("quality") can only occur when the processes that are responsible for creating the service or product are well understood and completely carried out. It has to be documented. Right or wrong, efficient or inefficient, the current process needs to be consistently followed to have stability. If we can translate this into healthcare, then we will at least have reliable outcomes, and humans crave reliability. Once the process is reliable, we venture to improve the process.

Returning to our example of the interactions between distribution and the OR, we would start with a detailed description of the process, including all the steps for the ordering clerk, instrument cleaning technician, supply clerk, physician, surgeon, anesthesiologist, prep nurse, OR nurse, transporter, and any additional support personnel. This provides a baseline from which to improve. Accept that this may not be the most efficient method, but at least everyone understands and completes the process as outlined. If the supply and distribution processes are followed by everyone in distribution, then the surgeries will be more likely to start on time and instrument- or supply-based infections will not occur. We have not "fixed" anything or changed a process to improve quality, but we have begun to standardize the process. Standardizing the process is the first step in creating lasting improvements.

We have established that creating lasting improvements in services requires a stable structure. Creating conformance to standards and consistency improves the customers' perceptions of the product. Still, it is important to keep in mind that consistency does not always equate to satisfaction.

- A four-hour wait at an emergency department may be highly consistent but not meet with customers' expectations of quality. Customers desire consistency and conformance to their standards.
- If 98 of every 100 customers receive a perfect x-ray exam, then the two that did not have a perfect exam had 100% defective exams.
- Gold-plated faucets, although aesthetically pleasing, do not clean hands better than chrome faucets. Customers may perceive gold plating to signal higher quality, but if the standard is clean hands, there is no difference in quality between gold and chrome.

Finally, there is a tendency to want to work on issues that bother us the most. Unfortunately, these may not be the issues that are costing the most or are the most inefficient. The FTS works first on the functions that likely have the greatest effect on the stability. The simple Pareto principle or "80/20 rule" will identify the top 20% of factors that generate the greatest costs or revenues for a process. These are the areas that will have the biggest payback for an organization and should be the first areas that should be reviewed. Here is where your real work begins. Using the steps that follow, you will develop an FTS for your organization and then use the SOAP (standardize, optimize, and align each process) method to create a stable foundation on which to build further process improvements.

Phase I: Developing the Functional Tree Structure Diagrams

The simplest way of explaining the FTS is that it is a method for reviewing an organization and its workings, starting from a high level and then going into more detailed descriptions of the tools, steps, people, and outputs involved in each process and subprocess. It is peeling back each successive layer of the onion, pausing at each layer to examine its functions, and (using the SOAP principle) working to standardize, optimize, and align the processes. For simplicity, we walk through the program at a department level, but understand that the program is intended to be used top down: from the highest administrator to the individual steps (processes) that produce some unit of good or service. Incidentally, the task of developing the FTS may start with a manager, but as the tasks become more narrowly defined in each successively detailed FTS diagram, the domain experts, the individual employees who are performing the tasks within a process, would be responsible for providing the detail regarding the processes. In addition, processes are further defined using the process maps and the written process descriptions as shown further in this book. We want the entire process to be visible to easily review the level of process standardization, optimization, and alignment.

We start with the actual or current functional tree. For all practical purposes, it resembles a traditional organizational chart but with one important distinction. This functional tree does not have people's names and titles but shows functions and measures. It is a *process* organizational chart.

The functions define specific operations at a high level. For example, a hospital, the highest level in this example, will have patient care, surgery, ancillary, support, and administrative functions at the second level. The functions can be broken into further detail. Patient care can be divided into intensive care, medical care, surgical care, and specialty care (e.g., maternity and newborn) (Figure 6.1).

Often, organizations base decisions on the units of output of each department's function. The outputs might be the number of tests run, procedures completed, rooms cleaned, or patients admitted or the number of patient days. These are important but incomparable across functions when managing

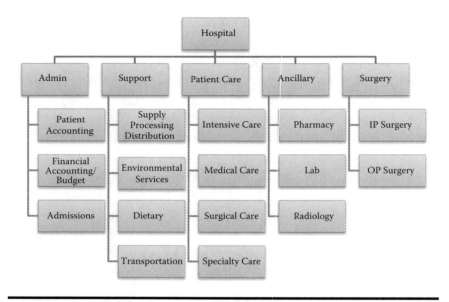

Figure 6.1   FTS: Level 1. IP, inpatient; OP, outpatient.

high-level functions. Every administrator eventually needs to have comparable and tangible measures that can be easily trended over time and can be compared to a budget or goal. The bottom line is financial performance to budget, and administrators should ask managers: "How are you doing against your financial budget?" Everything else flows from this question, assuming that the budget was carefully set. In addition, many highly rated organizations have cost budgets that vary according to their revenue, which takes into account the number of units produced.

The financial budget accounts for both the revenues generated and the costs incurred. Revenue shortfalls are caused by a reduction in demand, a competitive shift away from your organization, an inability to meet demand, or some combination of these three issues. Cost overruns are generally traced to unexpected rework, staffing greater than demand, unplanned problems, increased demand, or inefficiencies experienced. In these cases, the simple question—"How are you doing against your financial budget?"—begins the discussion that provides the information an administrator needs to know. It is also how we prefer to see organizations review and manage effort. With the FTS, we like to start with and report on basic measures. Administrators can compare functions using comparable measures that are tangible instead of attempting to compare the number of procedures run to the number of rooms cleaned. Examples of measures that are comparable across functional areas include

- Total revenue (if the function is a revenue-generating function)
- Total costs
- Number of full-time equivalents (FTEs)
- Patient satisfaction ratings of the area

Moreover, we can compare not only the functions within a hospital on these measures but also the hospitals. A hospital administrator can look at the costs, staffing, or revenue of the ancillary group of functions and compare that to the patient care function. From an administrator's perspective, managing at this level helps to put the importance of each function into perspective.

Although patient days, tests, blood draws, prescriptions filled, rooms cleaned, meals served, x-rays taken, admissions processed, and bills paid are all measures of the output of a function, they cannot be compared across functions. Is a meal served more or less important than a blood draw? Are rooms cleaned worth more than prescriptions filled? These are specific measures of output. They become important when we move to the second step of the FTS methodology and create current-state maps at the raw function level. But, before we begin to dissect individual functions, we need to know which functions provide the greatest opportunity to improve profitability, efficiency, and quality.

Consider again the FTS, now with total revenue and number of FTEs included (Figure 6.2). The FTS diagram with

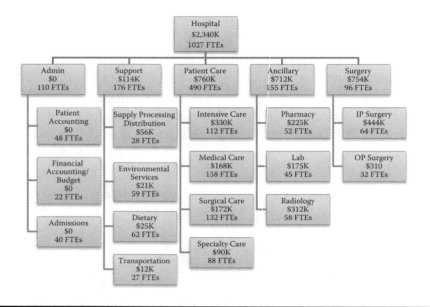

Figure 6.2   FTS: Level 1 showing revenue and FTEs.

these comparable measures shows that patient care generates one-third of the revenue and employs about half of the staff. Support of this function and alignment with all other functions is extremely important. Any improvements to process here will provide the greatest benefits. It is also important to know that there are a number of other ways to use the FTS. It can be shown with variance to budget, profitability, and labor performance to budget. In effect, it is a dashboard that visually describes how multiple functions are performing using a set of common and relevant measures.

Of course, we want to make sure that the processes within a function are stable and are adhered to universally. You can further refine your FTS by going deeper into each function and into the subfunctions that make up a function. For example, patient care has four primary functions, one of which is intensive care. Intensive care is made up of two nursing units with specific patient populations and goals: intensive care and cardiac care. These two units could be broken down further if they had functions within each unit that differed greatly, but for our example, each unit has measurable function-specific measures (patient days), and distinct boundaries can be drawn around each function.

Although not the most labor-intensive function, intensive care provides almost half of the revenue of the patient care function in our example. It may be the most efficiently run function within patient care, but as the revenue leader, it also provides the greatest opportunity for revenue loss if the function falters. Therefore, if we set total revenue as our measure of importance to the organization, we should flag patient care as first in line for further review in phase II. Similarly, intensive care can be broken into two distinct functions, the intensive care unit (ICU) and the cardiac care unit (CCU). Given its relative size, the CCU function would be the first to progress to phase II (Figure 6.3).

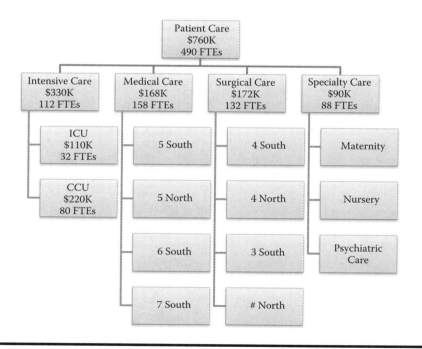

Figure 6.3   FTS: Level 2: Patient care services.

At this point, we have completed phase I. Keep in mind that other high-revenue functions can be identified and moved into phase II of the FTS at the same time. If our phase II review shows that intensive care is operating in a stable, optimized, and aligned fashion, the patient care manager can move on to the next-largest function.

At this last step, we begin to focus on the tasks employed in one of the CCU's processes. As Figure 6.4 shows, process 2 brings in the most revenue and has the greatest number of people and therefore the greatest opportunity to show improvements in process. With this process selected, we shift into phase II, the standardization, optimization, and alignment of process 2.

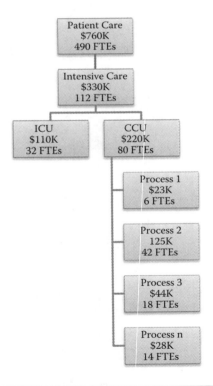

Figure 6.4   FTS: Level 3: CCU.

Note that your organization's FTS can be infinitely customized: The patient satisfaction, total costs, or employee satisfaction can also be included or substituted here as another way to identify the functions that should be worked on first. For instance, employee satisfaction is also a measure that is comparable across functions. Our observation is that functions with a high degree of employee satisfaction generally run efficiently and profitably, while functions with low employee satisfaction reflect the difficulties employees find in administering to their daily work flow and are generally less profitable. Your FTS can also display variance to budget, profitability, and labor performance to budget. In effect, it is a dashboard that visually describes how multiple functions are performing using a set of common and relevant measures.

FTS Phase II: Standardize, Optimize, and Align Each Process

In phase I, we charted an entire organization's worth of processes and the functions and measures of each. We identified those with the largest potential impact on revenue or cost; now, we want to understand the tasks and inputs currently used in the production of a good or service. In addition, the entire process is now visible at the macro level to everyone. Once the processes are charted using the FTS, we move into phase II of the FTS: We analyze the specific tasks that occur in each process. In phase II, we stabilize the process by first standardizing the process, aligning the process to fit with the processes that occur before and after, and then looking for opportunities to optimize the process. Figure 6.5 gives an overview of the entire process.

Throughout the standardize, optimize, and alignment steps of phase II, the team will be charged with identifying process *measurements* and providing *education* to the people performing and managing the tasks. There must be measurements for each task that describe the quantity and quality of the output. If no measurement can be found, it is likely that there is no output of value to the end customer, and the entire task could be eliminated. Education, especially in standardization, is intended to eliminate the variability in the way things are done. As output variability is the bane of consistency and quality, education is the cure used to reduce variation, improve consistency, and improve quality.

An issue faced by every department and team is that a hospital never shuts down. In some manufacturing organizations, there is planned downtime when plants and processes can be retooled and training can occur during halted production. In most healthcare settings, there is no scheduled downtime or plant shutdown to institute needed changes. The changes and improvements must occur while operations continue. This means that there will be added costs to continue operations as processes are reviewed, changed, taught, and measured. There are tools that can be used to implement change while operations continue. These include Taguchi robust engineering methods, single-minute change-of-die techniques, Six Sigma, Lean, and other techniques that often require process matter experts such as management engineers. The payback, of course, comes with the reduction in variation, which drives costly waste, error, and inefficiencies throughout the system. As the steps in this second phase of the FTS are implemented, understand that the process will likely suffer as additional resources are used to review and identify tasks that lead to instability.

Step 1: Document the Current State

Starting with the function in phase I that you flagged for immediate review, gather three to five process experts (staff who are engaged in the process day in and day out) and one individual experienced with implementing the FTS as the facilitator to create the current-state map. The current-state map visually displays all of the tasks completed in a process. It is a road map of the current tasks and decisions that must be made to complete the process that creates the desired output. It makes the process both visible (using a simplified flowchart) and numerical (by identifying the magnitude, frequency, and importance of each step in this one process).

The session will start by documenting the initial step: the action that begins the process. For example, in the CCU day-of-surgery process, the initiating step is when notification is received that a CCU patient will be going to surgery. In the discharge process, the initiating step is when the doctor's orders that the patient is to be moved to a step-down or primary care unit are received. From the initiating step, the team documents every step and decision using simple flowcharting techniques, trying to make the process as linear as possible. As a rule of thumb, activities or tasks that take more than ten minutes to complete should be broken down into smaller tasks (Figure 6.6).

Use the following steps to document the current state of the process you identified in phase I as needing immediate review:

A. Have your team create the current-state map.
    i. The team will make sure that the steps are appropriately sequenced based on how the process is currently done—not necessarily the "best" or most efficient sequence. This is to become the current-state map, and we recommend that before the team tries to improve on the process, the current process should be documented and stabilized.
    ii. For each process on the chart, the team will identify (alongside the task on the current-state map) who performs the tasks, where the task is performed, how long the task should take, and the frequency of the task per week or month. The team can also add other related remarks and information, such as required information and required supply. For the time standard, the

1: Document the Current State:

A. Create the current state process map

B. Document the "SMART" metrics that will be used to measure process performance, stability, and improvements

C. Collect historical data using the smart metrics (This will be used to measure progress and improvements)

D. Test each process in the current state map using the three questions—this eliminates all non-value added steps and helps to stabilize the process (at this point you have your "What" as in What you are doing)

E. Review and incorporate input from all staff engaged in the process

2: Standardize

A. Determine how everyone is performing each process and then standardize on one process (now you have the "How" as in How the process is supposed to be done)

B. Create a new Standardized Current State Map and detailed procedures manual that explains the tasks in the process (Appendixes A and B show examples of these)

C. Educate all employees on the "Hows" showing them the Stabilized process map

D. Start measuring, using the smart metrics, to get a baseline

3: Optimize

A. Look for ways to improve the efficiency of the process while not degrading the outputs— they still need to conform to or improve the customers' standards

B. Use the PI tools to reduce waste, improve consistency, reduce time, reduce costs

C. Create a new Standardized and Optimized State Map and update the detailed procedures

D. Educate all employees on the new aligned process showing them the Stabilized and Aligned process map

E. Continue measuring process performance and customer satisfaction using SMART metrics

4: Align

A. Obtain process specifications from the customers (internal and external) of our process

B. Review the standardized process map and look for ways to align the process so that the outputs conform to customer standards (quality)

C. Determine what changes to the inputs are needed to reduce variation in the outputs and communicate them to the upstream producers

D. Create a new Standardized, Optimized, and Aligned Process State Map and update the detailed procedures

E. Educate all employees on the new aligned process showing them the Stabilized and Aligned process map

F. Continue measuring using the smart metrics

Figure 6.5   FTS: Standardize, Optimize, Align.

team can use an estimated time or an actual standard time based on experts' experience using the DELPHI technique—a method of group decision making that involves gathering the judgment of experts.

B. Next, we need to determine an overall measure of the process's performance. This should be measured against the standards believed to be what the end customer desires. Examples of measures could be turnaround time, clarity of an x-ray, accuracy of measurements (i.e., intravenous bags have the correct solution at the correct concentration in the correct amount). Both quantity and quality measures are necessary for the process.

C. Collect historical data using the performance metrics so that you have a baseline to measure improvements made over time.

D. This next step is essential and begins the stabilization process. With the process map in hand, the process experts need to review each task in the process and ask the following three questions:

Q1: Does this step change the nature of the product/ service?

Q2: Is this step required by any credentialing or regulatory agency?

Q3: Will the patient/customer be willing to pay for this step?

If the answer is Yes (√) to any one of the three questions, the task should be kept. If these three criteria are not met, then the step is not required and should be eliminated. A new process map should be built without this step.

E. Once the first pass on documenting the current process has been completed, it is best to review the entire process with others to make sure that important steps have not been omitted and obtain buy-in from all participants on the current state. As always, strive for consensus among participants but take the majority opinion if the group cannot come to consensus.

CCU Care Process: Day of Surgery

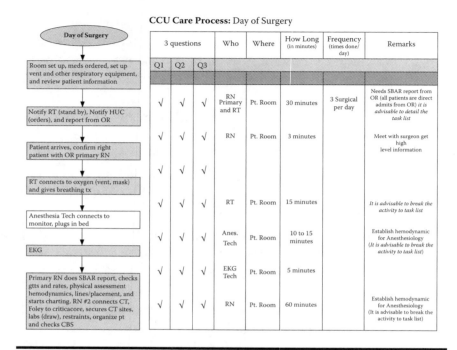

Figure 6.6   FTS: Current-state map of CCU.

Step 2: Standardize

After eliminating the non-value-added steps, it is time to standardize the process and initiate staff training. Even with the nonessential steps removed from the current-state map, the team has not arrived at a stable state. Within each task, there is likely to be variation in the ways individuals perform each task. To eliminate variation, the team must get everyone to follow the same method or use the same set of instructions. To do this, the process experts need to survey all of the people individually to understand specifically the actions they take during each step. What the process experts are likely to find is that everyone has their own method for performing each task. This team of process experts will standardize and document one method that all staff will use when performing each task. In simplistic terms, this is how the task should be performed by everyone doing the task. Although this seems to be a daunting process, the current-state map and task documentation become the detailed procedure manual needed for the Joint Commission (formerly the Joint Commission on Accreditation for Healthcare Organizations; JCAHO) and International Organization for Standardization (ISO) 9000.

The steps are straightforward:

A. Determine the tasks that staff use to perform each process. It is likely that individual staff members will perform tasks differently or in different sequences for each process.

   i. Document each task in the process shown in the current-state map. The form Process Description (Appendix B) is a tool that should be used to uniformly describe each task. In addition, this can be incorporated into or replace documentation of processes to meet JCAHO requirements (Figure 6.7).

   ii. When individual staff members perform a task differently or in different sequences, the process that most effectively and efficiently produces results with the least variation while conforming to customers' standards should be chosen. This becomes the "how" and is documented for reference, training, and retraining staff and for use in optimizing the process after the entire process has been stabilized.

B. Create a revised current-state map if needed.

C. Using the new standardized current-state map developed in step 1A and the detailed procedures developed in step 2A, educate all employees on how to carry out each task. The standardized process map and detailed procedures manual are the references each member of the staff must use to reduce variation and provide a consistently better product or service. It is good to practice or demonstrate the correct procedure to ensure that staff involved with a process understand how to correctly carry out the process.

Process Description		
Process Trait	**Vital Information**	**Explanation**
Process: Map:	(Example: Final Patient Prep) (Example: CCU Care Process – Day of Surgery)	Task or activity name in Process Map Name of the Process Map
Step: Created by: Date update:	(Example: 3.4) (Example: Barb Smith, RN and Nick Wilson, P.E.) Example: YYYY/MM/DD)	Step on Process Map Team who created the process description Date of most recent update
Process owner:	(Example: Mary Jones, RN/ Pre-Op)	Department and department manager where the process is done
Process description:	For example, in the process map you may have a three minute process called "Take vital signs of patient." The process description should be detailed and look like the following: 1. introduce yourself to the patient 2. ask the patient their name for verification 3. check the blood pressure and temperature apparatuses 4. take the blood pressure 5. chart 6. take temperature 7. chart 8. look at the patient for signs of skin or other disorders 9. chart 10. …	This is a written document that replaces the standard procedure manual. It must explain in great detail each small step in the process and the order it should be done in.
Performed by: Customer requirements: Measures:	(Example: Pre-surgery Nurse) (Example: 20 minutes before surgery, showing concern for the patient) For example: the % of surgeries with vital signs charted before the anesthesiology consult (Example: SMART Metrics)	The labor classification that performs this task A list of the requirements that the recipient requires for acceptable service The measurements used to determine process accuracy, reliability, and timeliness.
Average time:	(Example: 6 minutes per patient)	Time for
Materials needed:	(Example: Electronic chart, blood pressure cuff, digital thermometer)	A list of materials needed to complete the process
Next step in the process:	(Example: Anesthesiologist/Patient Consult)	

Figure 6.7   FTS: Process description.

D. Start measuring using SMART (simple, measurable, accurate and actionable, reliable and relevant, timely) metrics to obtain a baseline of how the standardized process is working. Everyone in the department should know the metrics used to monitor the performance of the processes on which they work.

It is possible that the team or department will want to create training materials and might request the assistance of the education department experts. It is also advisable to have a third party evaluate the materials for accuracy, simplicity, and teachability. All personnel affected by this process up to the department's director should fully understand the process and the metrics being used to monitor the performance of the process. When the materials are ready, a training plan should be implemented addressing who will train, who will be trained, the length of training, and mode of training (classroom hours, hands-on learning). Finally, it is best to have a member from the original team volunteer to train the staff and to maximize staff engagement (Figure 6.8).

Step 3: Optimize

The focus during this step is optimizing the tasks within your process and not to optimize the overall process. To reiterate a constant theme throughout the FTS method, you need to stabilize a process before working on process improvement; use one of the traditional improvement methods, such as Quality Function Deployment TRIZ,* TQM (total quality management), Six Sigma, Lean, and so on. There are tools that can be used to optimize a task and are shown in the following material, but traditional improvement methods are best used when working on stabilized processes.

---

* TRIZ is a problem-solving, analysis, and forecasting tool derived from the study of patterns of invention.

Implementation Plan

Project Name

Action Plan

Training

Activity Description	Start	End	Required Resources	Responsible	Accountable	Status	Remarks
Training Activity Description							
Design and produce training materials			Education Department	Process Owner	Department Dir.		
Define method of training (classroom and direct observation and feedback)			Education Department	Team	Process owner		
Identify trainers				Team	Process owner		
Train the trainers				Team/facilitator	Process owner		
Complete few dry runs				Team/facilitator	Process owner		
Finalize and approve trainers				Process owner	Department Dir.		
Group department staff							
Assign trainer to each group							
Determine reward for high performing group							
Establish performance metrics for each team and staff			Department Dir.	FTS facilitator			
Generate weekly report of each group and staff progress			Department Dir.	FTS facilitator			
Celebrate each team and team members on a weekly basis to keep high momentum			Department Dir.	FTS facilitator			
Continue the training (class, reinforcement), side-by-side work and observation, celebration and recognition for the first 3 months			Department Dir.	FTS facilitator	Process owner		

Figure 6.8   FTS: Example training and implementation plan.

In the optimized step, the team will look for improvements in the tasks that are easy to implement and affect only the task within the overall process. This might reduce variation in the outputs or reduce waste. Once the tasks have been reviewed and optimized, the overall process is stable—or at least more stable—and true process improvement, lasting process improvement, can begin. Let us look at the final step in the SOAP method.

A. Review each task in the process following the updated process map and task descriptions.
   i. Are there ways to improve the efficiency of the process while not reducing the outputs?
   ii. Are there tasks that can be combined?
   iii. Are there decisions that can be eliminated?
      As these tasks are being reviewed and changed, keep in mind that the output must at least conform to customers' standards (cost improvements) or exceed customers' standards by improving the process.
B. Using process improvement techniques on the recently standardized and aligned process and with the help of a process engineer or consultant, the team can look at one of two types of improvement processes:
   i. Change one variable and determine the outcome (this is known as a heuristic method) before adding on a second or third process change. This is called one *factor* at a time. Alternatively, it is better to use classic design-of-experiments techniques.
   ii. Deploy the classic design-of-experiments process to determine the relationship between outputs to the optimum level of each key performance input variable.
   iii. Use affinity diagrams, interrelationship diagraphs, brainstorming, and any of the Six Sigma, Lean, or Continuous Quality Improvement (CQI) tools or techniques.

C. Create a new stabilized, optimized, and aligned process state map and update the detailed procedures. Any improvements will need to be documented, taught, and measured using the tools and techniques previously presented.

D. Educate all employees on the new aligned process showing them the stabilized and aligned process map.

E. Continue measuring using the SMART metrics.

Step 4: Align

The final step of phase II is to align. Standardizing and optimizing your process will go a long way in reducing variation and increasing customer satisfaction. However, the process is still not completely stable. The next step is to align the output of your process with the standards set by your customer. Customers may be another process within the same department, a process in the next department, or the end customer, the patient. The alignment process may lead to identification of additional tasks that are not required by the customer of the process or requirements that have been previously unfulfilled, both of which will change the process map as new tasks are added or removed from the process map and new procedures are documented and taught. With previously unmet requirements brought to light, new SMART measures need to be initiated and monitored. In these cases, it is advisable to return to the standardize step to ensure that procedures are documented and taught to all staff.

The following are the steps to take during alignment:

A. Obtain process specifications. If quality is "conformance to standards," then we need to know what the next customer's standards are. The next customer may be another process within the same department, a process in the next department, or the end customer, the patient.

i. With the customers' standards in hand, review the standardized process map and your current SMART metrics for your process. Identify unmet requirements or requirements for which your process provides a product or service with excessive variation.

ii. Are there simple changes to your process that will help to improve your output so that it aligns and conforms to your customers' standards? If not, now is *not* the time to embark on a quality improvement project. You are still on the road to stabilization, and improvement should occur after stabilization.

B. Review the standardized and optimized process map and look for ways to align the process so that the outputs conform to customer standards (quality). What steps need to be changed to meet customer expectations? Consider the delivery time, quantity delivered, and attributes of the product or service that will affect the outputs of the next process. Are there simple changes to the inputs that would reduce variation in the outputs?

C. Ideally, we would also like to receive inputs to our process (the goods and services that become the inputs to our processes and inevitably shape the outputs) that conform to our standards and have minimal variation. If the current state of the inputs received significantly affects the outputs of your process—if they do not conform to reasonable standards—then your requirements must be communicated to the upstream producers through written input specifications.

D. Create a new stabilized, optimized, and aligned process state map and update the detailed procedures. Update the detailed procedures. Document any changes to the inputs that will reduce variation in the outputs.

E. Any improvements will need to be documented, taught, and measured using the tools and techniques previously presented. Educate all employees on the new aligned process, showing them the standardized, optimized, and aligned process map and new procedure documentation.

F. Again, review and revise if necessary your SMART metrics. Publish them for all to see.

The example in Figure 6.9 shows the refined process state map, often referred to as the "future-state" process map. This is the newly designed process after unwarranted steps are removed and processes are standardized, optimized, and aligned. It is now considered "stabilized" to denote that the process has gone through the steps of the FTS and is ready for process improvements.

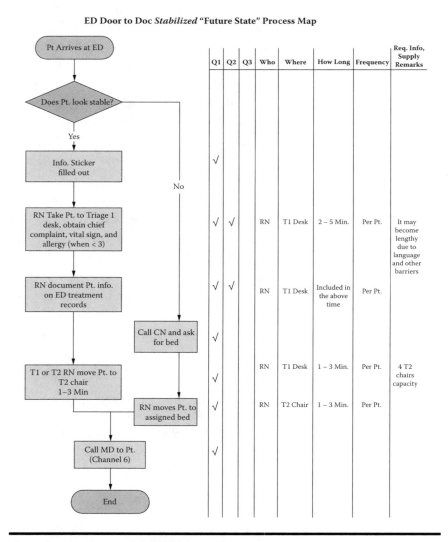

ED Door to Doc *Stabilized* "Future State" Process Map

Figure 6.9   FTS: Stabilized future-state process map.

Chapter 7

Selecting a Process Improvement Tool

Introduction

The overall picture we have painted is that to sustain operational improvements you first need to have a stable structure before you can improve processes. Once you have a stable structure, you keep it stable by managing the performance, using SMART (simple, measurable, accurate and actionable, reliable and relevant, timely) metrics, and supporting the structure that keeps operations stable and focused on improvement. This book has shown how to produce a stable structure using the functional tree structure (FTS). Managing performance and providing a supportive structure will help to solidify the culture of quality needed for an organization to grow (Figure 7.1).

There are many positive outcomes of instituting FTS in a healthcare operation or, for that matter, any type of for-profit or nonprofit organization:

- Under FTS, everyone knows what is expected of them.

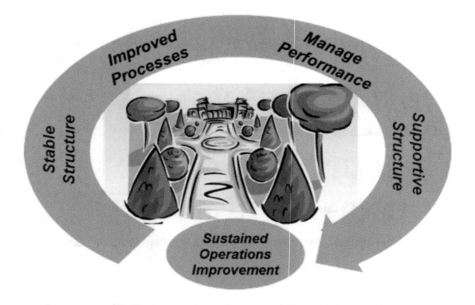

Figure 7.1 Understanding "My Process."

- Under FTS, everyone knows how to do the task and why.
  - Leaders are not managing people but managing processes.
  - Leaders are the educators and trainers.
- FTS creates orders and promotes discipline.
- FTS creates a lockstep environment.
  - Everyone walks the same way and moves in the same direction.
- FTS creates and nurtures a new culture.
- FTS creates a supportive environment for the workforce.
- FTS nurtures pride of workmanship.
- FTS nurtures innovative thoughts and futuristic approaches to problem solving by continuously asking what, why, where, who, when, how, and how often.
- FTS creates a profound understanding of a system's operations by illuminating the intricacies of all its interdependent parts and subsystems.
- FTS creates organizational strategic agility to respond to new market demands in a swift manner.

- FTS enhances the opportunity for positive impact on operations effectiveness and efficiency by changing exhausting work environments to exhilarating work environments and engaging staff members' innovative imagination by asking how to do it better.
- FTS creates a motivating and engaging work environment by nurturing, encouraging skill mastery, fostering teamwork and team membership, providing meaningful work, and realigning performance and outcome incentives.
- FTS reduces conflicts in the work environment by setting clear process boundaries and work domains.
- FTS nurtures, enhances, and encourages horizontal problem solving.
- FTS decreases "within" and "between" variation while enhancing outcome reliability.

Having gone through the FTS program and stabilized at least one process, organizations should continue to stabilize processes until 80% of the staff have gone through the entire process. The stabilization of processes, elimination of unneeded steps, and consistency derived from the documentation and education will make remarkable improvements in quality without even starting to implement process improvements. At this time, you have completed your FTS and identified the dominant functions of your department or organization, documented and educated the "what" (what you are doing) and "how" (how you are doing it); the processes are stable and being measured. Now, it is time to expand the implementation of the FTS.

With the FTS completed in the departments that provide 80% of the organization's revenue or 80% of the organization's cost, the organization's leadership should ask, How can we do better? How can we surpass our competitors? or How can we realign operations, manage costs, increase revenues so that we create a healthy bottom line? This begins the operations improvement phase, the third phase in the process.

To reiterate, phase I makes the process visual using an FTS diagram and selects the processes that will have the greatest effect on quality. Phase II stabilizes the processes, eliminates waste, and helps everyone use the same processes. At this point, the third phase—actual process improvement—begins. The first step (and likely the step that everyone has been waiting to start) is to look for opportunities to improve on the *stabilized* processes. Engage staff by having them continuously ask, How can we do it better? By focusing on the intrinsic value of their performance and not the extrinsic worth of their output, all staff have a stake in fine-tuning their individual contributions to the entire process.

Management's role here is to identify and prioritize departments and processes with highest opportunities for improvements in costs, operations, or quality. With processes identified for improvement, the next step is to select the most appropriate process improvement method. To help you select the best concept, we provide a brief introduction to Continuous Quality Improvement (CQI), Six Sigma, and Lean concepts. CQI focuses on identifying and implementing improvements. Six Sigma incorporates project management techniques and is used in conjunction with Lean tools, which are effective in eliminating waste. There are many handbooks, pamphlets, and articles available for those interested reading in more depth, so the primer that follows is merely a guide to your possibilities from this point.

Continuous Quality Improvement

The CQI concept follows Shewhart's PDCA (Plan, Do, Check (or Study), and Act). The approach was later modified, updated, and perfected by Dr. W. Edwards Deming while helping Japanese manufacturing recover after World War II. Deming enhanced the CQI concept by introducing his 14 points and what he termed *scientific management* and his *System of*

Deming/Shewhart: (PDCA) Cycle[1]

1. **PLAN**: Plan a change or test how something works by identifying What, When, Where, Who, Why, How, and How Often.

2. **DO**: Carry out the plan, small test of change, and collect data.

3. **CHECK** (alternatively "Study"): Analyze data and review the results. What did you find out?

4. **ACT**: Decide what actions should be taken to improve, standardize, and implement the new process.

[1] Image found at: http://en.wikipedia.org/wiki/PDCA from *The Improvement Guide: A Practical Approach to Enhancing Organizational Performance*, 2nd Edition by Gerald J. Langley, Ronald Moen, Kevin M. Nolan, Thomas W. Nolan, Clifford L. Norman, Lloyd P. Provost Published by Jossey-Bass ISBN 978-0-470-19241-2.

Figure 7.2   Deming/Shewhart PDCA cycle.

Profound Knowledge (SoPK). Figures 7.2 and 7.3, respectively, provide quick schematics of the PDCA cycle and the SoPK.*

A multitude of tools exist for use during CQI projects; these tools all require rigorous project management discipline and a solid understanding of statistical methods to ensure success of the project's outcome. "Profound knowledge" is akin to Socrates's "advanced understanding." He explained knowledge to Plato using three levels of understanding: the *elementary* is the "know what" stage, the *intermediate* is the "know how" stage, and the *advanced* stage is when you understand or "know why" something is done. Figure 7.4 shows this hierarchy.

Deming's SoPK builds on this philosopher's epistemology of knowledge and was also profoundly influenced by C. I. Lewis's book *Mind and the World Order*[1] through its introduction of conceptual pragmatism. SoPK is a rational and logical extension of the Taylor theory of scientific management, which combines the human aspect with the mechanistic methods

---

* Image found at http://www.3sigma.com/demings-system-of-profound-knowledge/.

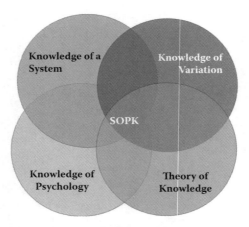

Figure 7.3 Deming System of Profound Knowledge.

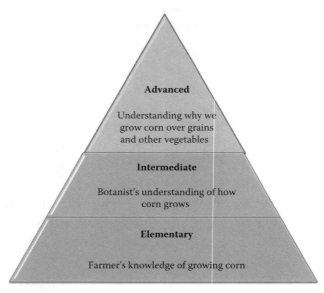

Figure 7.4 Socrates's advanced understanding.

where work is done. SoPK can be further defined by looking at the four principles:

1. *Knowledge of Variation*: There are a number of causes of variation in quality. The knowledge of the type of variation can be seen using statistical sampling techniques.

There are two primary types of variation that statistical sampling can capture: random or common cause variation and special cause variation. Special cause variation refers to any variation for which the cause can be traced to man, machine, method, or Mother Nature. In addition, there can be variation within the process (repeatability) or between processes (reproducibility). Both are deadly to quality improvement. In achieving profound knowledge, understanding the types and sources of variation is imperative to improve.

2. *Knowledge of a System (Appreciation of a System)*: Georg Wilhelm Friedrich Hegel, a German philosopher, defined system knowledge as thoroughly understanding the network of interdependent parts working together to attain the goals or objectives of the system. Likewise, Deming advised understanding a system in totality, the appropriateness of each of the independent parts, and their roles in system functionalities. This includes the suppliers, producers, and customers of the system. The FTS helps to describe and communicate the network of interdependent parts.

3. *Knowledge of Psychology*: Human psychology or human nature can have a significant effect, both positive and devastatingly negative, on the outcome of any process and therefore is important to consider whenever processes are improved. Everything from organizational structure to individuals' mindsets can have an effect on process improvement success. Misconceptions, miscommunications, unfocused or unshared goals, unrealistic expectations, and poor management can all wreak havoc on the most prevalent and important resource used in patient care: people. We advise organizations first to stabilize the functional structure and then deploy appropriate psychological concepts. There are many books and theories on what makes humans work productively together that can be used here.

4. *Theory of Knowledge*: Knowledge is useless if it is not transferable. Deming's point here is that the SoPK requires that practitioners transfer knowledge to staff in a way that is understandable. Deep understanding of a concept does not necessarily happen in a classroom or on receipt of a certificate. The introduction of the greatest advancements has been delayed or lost when the brilliant inventor could not effectively communicate knowledge. Teaching techniques that consider individual differences in learning style and incorporate best teaching practices, such as visualization, repetition, and Socratic methods, can improve the knowledge transfer process.

Deming used his 14 points as a method to aid in improvement processes. These are a shorthand that facilitates process and organization improvement. The 14 points are as follows[*]:

1. Create constancy of purpose toward improvement of product and service, with the aim to become competitive, to stay in business, and to provide jobs.
2. Adopt the new philosophy. We are in a new economic age. Western management must awaken to the challenge, must learn their responsibilities, and must take on leadership for change.
3. Cease dependence on inspection to achieve quality. Eliminate the need for massive inspection by building quality into the product in the first place.
4. End the practice of awarding business based on a price tag. Instead, minimize total cost. Move toward a single supplier for any one item, creating a long-term relationship of loyalty and trust.

---

[*] From Deming, W. Edwards (2011, November 9). *Out of the Crisis* (pp. 23–24). Cambridge, MA: MIT Press. https://www.deming.org/theman/theories/fourteenpoints

5. Improve constantly and forever the system of production and service, to improve quality and productivity, and thus constantly decrease costs.
6. Institute training on the job.
7. Institute leadership. The aim of supervision should be to help people and machines and gadgets do a better job. Supervision of management is in need of overhaul, as well as supervision of production workers.
8. Drive out fear so that everyone may work effectively for the company.
9. Break down barriers between departments. People in research, design, sales, and production must work as a team to foresee problems of production and usage that may be encountered with the product or service.
10. Eliminate slogans, exhortations, and targets for the workforce that ask for zero defects and new levels of productivity. Such exhortations only create adversarial relationships because the bulk of the causes of low quality and low productivity belong to the system and thus lie beyond the power of the workforce.
    a. Eliminate work standards (quotas) on the factory floor. Substitute with leadership.
    b. Eliminate management by objective. Eliminate management by numbers and numerical goals. Instead, substitute with leadership.
11. Remove barriers that rob the hourly worker of the worker's right to pride of workmanship. The responsibility of supervisors must be changed from sheer numbers to quality.
12. Remove barriers that rob people in management and in engineering of their right to pride of workmanship. This means, inter alia, abolishment of the annual or merit rating and of management by objectives.
13. Institute a vigorous program of education and self-improvement.
14. Put everybody in the company to work to accomplish the transformation. The transformation is everybody's job.

The Seven Deadly Diseases* describes the most serious barriers that management potentially faces within an organization. Outlined next are Deming's Seven Deadly Diseases of Management, as well as an explanation of each.

1. Lack of constancy of purpose to plan product and service that will have a market and keep the company in business and provide jobs.

   As long as the focus is on short-term thinking, management will fail to plan adequately. Without good long-term planning, worker efforts will be irrelevant: *Total quality management (TQM)* cannot be a fad because long-term forward progress should always be the ultimate goal for any organization.

2. Emphasis on short-term profits and short-term thinking.

   Short-term thinking is the opposite of constancy of purpose and is fueled by bankers and owners pushing for dividends. Boosting short-term profits is easier as it typically involves the cutting of any expense related to the long term: training, quality assurance management, and maintenance.

3. Evaluation of performance, merit rating, or annual review.

   Management by objective, on a go/no-go basis, without a method for accomplishment of the objective, is the same thing as management by fear. The essential problem with merit systems is that they reward results rather than process improvement; results will almost always have a large amount of system luck in the mix. Some managers want to reward people who cooperate more or who seem to have better attitudes and will insist that they can recognize the people who are most cooperative and have the highest work ethic. Instead, managers should understand that

---

* From Deming, W. Edwards (2011, November 9). W. Edwards Deming's Fourteen Points and Seven Deadly Diseases of Management in *Out of the Crisis* (pp. 97–98). Cambridge, MA: MIT Press.

the best way to develop cooperation is by focusing on the nature of the work environment, not monetary rewards.

4. Mobility of management and job hopping.

The simplest and yet one of the most deadly of quality systems management diseases, management mobility (or when top management changes organizations every three or four years), means continuous improvement efforts will be broken and disjointed as new leaders come onboard. With changes in leadership, there is a change in management philosophy. Managers who have an eye on the next promotion want results—now—to gain the next rung on the ladder.

5. Management exclusively by visible figures, with little or no consideration for figures that are unknown or unknowable.

Some facts are simply unknowable. Knowing this, Deming insisted that leaders must still make decisions and manage a situation. This leads to a basic dilemma: How do you know what would have happened if you had kept on your prior course? How do you put a dollar value on the customer loyalty won through quality improvement efforts? The answer is that you cannot because these numbers are unknowable—and this must be taken into consideration.

6. Excessive medical costs.

For the economy as a whole, healthcare as a percentage of overall expenditures has steadily risen for decades, which gradually pushes numerous businesses into a state of crisis. Potentially, the only remedy for this disease would be a political system that attempts to reform healthcare.

7. Excessive costs of liability, swelled by lawyers who work on contingency fees.

Deming frequently blamed America's lawyers in part for the problems of American business. The United States has more lawyers per capita than any other country in the world, and these lawyers spend much of their professional time finding people to sue. Like healthcare costs in item 6, Deming believed the remedy to this disease will probably have to come from the government.

Six Sigma

Inconsistent results and haphazard CQI implementations in the 1980s led engineer Bill Smith of Motorola to create a more scientific methodology for approaching process improvement. He created the Six Sigma concept, which Allied Signal and GE later used to reduce costs and increase market share. Six Sigma is a method of improving product or service quality by focusing on decreasing variation in the key input variables and processes. The following is a simple overview of the benefits of the Six Sigma method:

- Six Sigma uses a more defined and rigorous project management approach over traditional operations improvement processes.
- Six Sigma also introduced a more rigorous set of statistical tools and concepts to ensure that the improvement team followed a scientific approach to operations improvement. In our mind, Six Sigma is CQI on statistical steroids accompanied with a well-defined project management process.
- Six Sigma focuses on short-term and immediate gains.
- Six Sigma improves quality and operations by decreasing variability in the key process input variables (KPIVs).
- Six Sigma frequently uses one of two main methods:
  - DMAIC (Define, Measure, Analyze, Improve, and Control) for existing processes
    - **Define:** To define project boundaries
    - **Measure:** Identify potential performance variables $(Y = f(x))$

- **Analyze:** Determine critical performance factors
- **Improve:** Redesign major process to meet customer requirements and test new process performance
- **Control:** Implement and hardwire redesign process
  - DMADV (Define, Measure, Analyze, Design, and Verify) for new processes

We prefer the DMAIC method after the FTS has been rolled out. It fits well with the what and how concept previously described in the FTS. After the process improvement team answers the question, Why are we producing this product or service? then the team can deploy DMAIC to improve the product or service. Again, we can base the design of the new process using customers' specifications by capturing the voice of the customers (VoC) and using quality functional deployment.

Lean

Lean improves value to customers by eliminating waste in the processes. It is based on the simple equation *Value = Quality/Cost.*

Improving quality requires a thorough examination of the operations and underlying processes to learn what portion of the operations or processes creates poor quality. Lean is an approach focused on decreasing waste and thereby providing greater value to the customer. The Toyota Lean production model identifies seven types of waste (Figure 7.5).

The Toyota production model is the source of many of the Lean tools. Toyota structured these tools for use in every operational situation. A brief introduction to these tools is helpful when looking at ways to improve processes. We begin with a tool that we recommend as the starting point for process improvement methods.

Categories of Waste	
1. Overproduction, excess capacity, overstaffing to demand	
2. Correction, correcting any error or steps not done before	
3. Processing, over process, unnecessary steps and review	
4. Inventory, any more stock than minimum needed to get the job done	
5. Waiting, for signature or an appointment	
6. Motion, any patient transfer, supply relocation, which does not add value	
7. Material and information movement, any nonessential transport is waste	

Figure 7.5   Lean categories of waste.

5S Concept

5S is an engineering approach to reduce waste and optimize productivity through maintaining an orderly and organized workplace. 5S uses visual cues to achieve more consistent and improved operational results. Implementation of this method "cleans up" and organizes the workplace basically in its existing configuration, and it is typically the first Lean method that organizations should implement. Figure 7.6 enumerates the 5S steps. The description of each step follows:

> **Sort:** Sort is the first step in 5S implementation. During this step, a team will filter through all workplace inventories and tools to identify needless items, redundancies, and hazards. Clutter impairs productivity, creates

Japanese word	English translation
1. Seiri	Sort
2. Seiton	Straighten/Store
3. Seiso	Sanitize/Sweep
4. Seiketsu	Standardize
5. Shitsuke	Sustain

Figure 7.6   Lean 5S concept.

hazards, frustrates personnel, and limits job performance. Clutter is often built up during operations, especially if upkeep and organization are not built into the standard process. During the sort stage, each item's purpose, uniqueness, and importance to job function should be evaluated to provide criteria for removal. Unnecessary items will then become more obvious, including duplications, outdated items, obsolete items, and damaged items.

Check what is needed and then eliminate all nonessential tools and materials from the workplace:

1. Separate unnecessary items, fill in and attach a red tag, validate status, remove or relocate.
2. Complete and attach a yellow tag on items that "may be" necessary; red tag them after 30 days of inactivity.
3. Tag and store items currently not being used but that may be needed later in a designated offline location.
4. Involve a neutral assessor for unbiased views

Straighten/Store: Set an optimal storage place for each item based on the frequency of use in the workplace. Use visual management to facilitate quick observation and upkeep of par levels.

Sanitize/Sweep: Make it a practice to always keep the work area and equipment clean. Identify who is responsible for cleaning and create a cleaning schedule. Deploy SMART metrics showing the who, what, and when cleaning occurs and evaluate continuously.

The next two steps are focused on sustaining the new supply organization and cleanliness of the workplace.

Standardize: Improve and maintain the first 3Ss through establishing visual controls, standard procedures, and checklists for all to maintain a neat, tidy, and functional work area that facilitates workers' access to materials and tools at appropriate par levels. This will require that

an accurate and acceptable economic reorder point is
set and calculated using the minimum acceptable number of items before reorder and lead time required to
receive items.

Sustain: To ensure sustainability, create a responsibility
matrix that defines every member's role and responsibilities. A responsibility matrix becomes the system that
monitors the workplace cleanliness.

Standard of Work

Another tool that supports process improvements is the "standard of work" (SoW). This tool is frequently used by Lean
practitioners. The SoW creates a solid understanding of the
way in which work is done while demonstrating the sequence
of the tasks and activities that yields the defined outcome. To
differentiate between SoW and work standard, we provide the
following definitions:

a. A *work standard* is a time and motion study term that
defines the allotted time for a specific task or activity to
be done.
b. An SoW is a Lean term that describes a sequence of
activities and associated allotted time to complete the job.
This will provide a context for process improvement and
elimination of the non-value-added steps.

In healthcare, most often Lean practitioners use the standard
operating procedure (SOP) format instead of the commonly used
format in Lean manufacturing. Figure 7.7 provides an example.

The SoW is an important tool for operators and management during continuous improvement. It enhances the ability
of the process owner or operators to mitigate problems and
process constraints. Figure 7.8 provides an example of a completed hybrid SoW activity map for a triage intake.

	Hybrid SoW Template					
	SoW "Activity Map" Name					
Rank	Activity Description	Must Do	Like to Do	Nice to Do	Required Time	Remarks
1						
2						
3						
4						
5						
6						
7						
8						
9						
10						
11						
12						
13						
14						
15						

Figure 7.7   Lean standard of work worksheet.

Value Stream Map

Value stream mapping (VSM) refers to a graphic representation of the trail of activities that occur from the moment a request is made for a service until the moment that request is fulfilled. It is a pictorial presentation of end-to-end service delivery process. By definition, VSM is a high-level and complete picture of a process that has been selected for improvement. It is a helpful tool to be deployed at the beginning of a Lean project to ensure a complete understanding of the process and to make the process visible from beginning to end, including

Organization Name

Triage Hybrid SoW "Activity Map"

Rank	Activity Description	Must Do	Like to Do	Nice to Do	Time Study 1	2	3	4	5	6	7	8	9	10	Best	Avg	Remarks
1	Chief complaint	✓															
2	EKG		✓														
3	Allergy	✓															
4	Meds.		✓														
5	Patient history		✓														
6	Vital sign	✓															
7	Primary doctor		✓														
8	Height and weight "Adult"		✓														
9	Height and weight "Children"	✓															
10	Last menstrual period			✓													
11	Depression			✓													
12	Suicidal			✓													
13	T. B. questions	✓															
14	Kids immunization		✓														
15	Finger stick			✓													
16	Tetanus status			✓													
17	More questions about chief complaint			✓													

Figure 7.8 Lean standard of work example.

Continued

18	Look at patient		✓											
19	Neurological assessment			✓										
20	Input data into computer		✓											
21	Patient education				✓									
22	Document education				✓									
23	Medicate patient				✓									
24	Call charge nurse to ask what is going on				✓									
25	Review patient documents				✓									
26	Specimen collection				✓									
27	Glucose check				✓									
28	Animal form is given				✓									
29	Suture removal				✓									
30	Document suture removal				✓									
31	Put patient on oxygen			✓										
32	Listen and comfort				✓									
33	Consult family				✓									
34	Service recovery				✓									

Figure 7.8 (*Continued*) Lean standard of work example.

both value-added and non-value-added time, including wait, transport, queuing, and check. Finally, it provides a value for a specific efficiency metric named the process efficiency percentage (Figure 7.9).

Why should we use VSM:

- To create a high-level view of the steps and activities in the process
- To identify areas of concerns and to recognize high-level opportunities
- To modify the scope of the improvement activities
- To create a pictorial presentation of all activities that contribute to the final product
- To learn more about all processes that produce the complete service/product
- To create a complete picture of end-to-end processes
- To identify wastes and processes for improvement
- To create a focused scope for the improvement project

Endnote

1. Lewis, C.I. (1956). *Mind and the World Order: Outline of a Theory of Knowledge*. New York: Dover Publications.

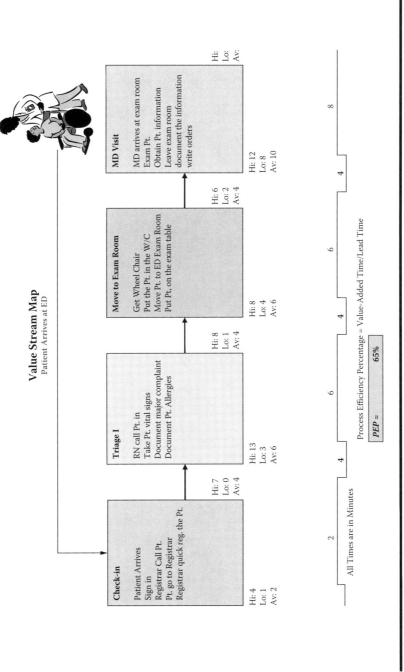

Figure 7.9 Example value stream map. W/C = wheelchair.

Chapter 8

Wrapping Up

> Vision without action is daydream. Action without vision is nightmare.
>
> **—Japanese proverb**

One observation that we can make based on over 20 years of observation within the healthcare system is that many people understand part of what their organization is doing, but that a profound understanding of the complete operations is held by few people. Although Continuous Quality Improvement (CQI), Six Sigma, Lean, and Lean Six tools and concepts can help support process improvements, when two-thirds of healthcare process improvement projects in the healthcare industry fail to sustain their gains beyond six to nine months, it should be evident that something is wrong with the way that they are implemented. Process improvement tools have been shown to be more effective, and improvements have been longer lasting, in manufacturing and other industries. It would appear that they have been less effective in healthcare overall. That is not to say that they have been totally ineffective. There are many examples of process improvement projects in healthcare that have provided lasting improvements. Chapter 2 identified the factors that led to success and failure of a project, with process instability, complexity, and variability as the primary drivers.

In all sectors of the business economy and especially in healthcare, organizations try to improve their environment to win market share from competitors. They try to carve a niche, differentiate their services, or claim higher quality and better outcomes. Often, changes made in healthcare systems are done at the department or task level and may not be integrated into the larger strategic direction of the organization. As we have described, functional tree structures (FTSs) help ensure that everyone who works within a process (and that is every *productive* person in an organization) has profound knowledge of both the "what" and the "how" of a process, setting up healthcare organizations for long-term success. It is the responsibility of the organization's management to make sure that the what is relevant in the economy and that the how is done in a competitive manner. This may include identifying changes in the environment and directing the production of goods and services only after first demonstrating a complete understanding of the current state of the organization's performance. They need to communicate a what that makes sense in the current and future environment and facilitate the how. They need to initiate changes based on a well-thought-out vision while understanding the current state of organizational performance using a profound knowledge of what and how. Otherwise, their decisions will be poor and will lead to organizational decline.

In healthcare, FTS works on the root cause of many of the process improvement failures—the unstable base operations on which improvements are too often precariously built. And, no matter how robust the improvement process was, when the underlying operations shift or crumble, the improvements are the first tasks that are pushed aside. It is important to reiterate what FTS strives to do. The positive outcomes of instituting FTS in a healthcare operation are the following:

- Under FTS, everyone knows what is expected of them.
- Under FTS, everyone knows how to do the task and why.
  - Leaders are not managing people but managing processes.
  - Leaders are the educators and trainers.
- FTS creates orders and promotes discipline.
- FTS creates a lockstep environment: Everyone walks the same way and moves in the same direction.
- FTS creates and nurtures a new culture.
- FTS creates a supportive environment for the workforce.
- FTS nurtures pride of workmanship.
- FTS nurtures innovative thoughts and futuristic approaches to problem solving by continuously asking what, why, where, who, when, how, and how often.
- FTS creates a profound understanding of systems' operations by illuminating the intricacies of all the interdependent parts and subsystems.
- FTS creates organization strategic agility to respond to new market demands in a swift manner.
- FTS enhances the opportunity for positive impact on operations effectiveness and efficiency by changing exhausting work environments to exhilarating work environments and engaging the innovative imagination of the staff by asking, "How can I do it better?"
- FTS creates a motivating and engaging work environment by nurturing, encouraging skill mastery, fostering teamwork and team membership, providing meaningful work, and realigning performance and outcome incentives.
- FTS reduces conflicts in the work environment by setting clear process boundaries and work domains.
- FTS encourages horizontal problem solving.
- FTS decreases "within" and "between" variation while enhancing outcome reliability.

Appendix A: Guide to Creating a Process Map

A process map is a means used to document work practices and convey information about a process. Process maps are important because they help find ways to simplify, streamline, and redesign the process. During the creation of a process map, a team familiar with the process will agree on the steps of the process, determine which activities have an impact on process performance, identify data collection points, and when done, use it to train others on the process.

The objective of creating a process map is to help teams see how a whole process works, including the flow of the steps, events, people, and materials and their relationships to each other. It helps to identify problem areas, bottlenecks, or instances in processes where non-value-adding work is performed. In addition, it shows critical points in a process and where teams can collect data.

The first process maps that are created as the "current-state" process maps inevitably are improved to show the "ideal" or "future-state" map, in which the flow of the process, from start to finish, has been simplified, streamlined, or redesigned.

But, before creating a process map we need to have a definition of a process:

A process is a systematic, sequenced series of inter-dependent actions that, at every stage, consume one or more resources to convert inputs into outputs.

We also need to know why process is important.

1. Outcomes, and especially predictable outcomes, are the result of the transformation of inputs and processes. Achieving consistent results requires consistent inputs processed through a stable process.
2. The only way to change or improve the results is to change the input or processes.

Ironically, we often believe the outcomes will be what we want them to be without considering the inputs and process when, in truth, every process is perfectly designed to produce what it is producing. If it takes three minutes for an egg to become hard boiled, the methods have to change to obtain a boiled egg in two minutes. Additional equipment, higher temperatures, or semicooked eggs would need to be introduced to create a new process: the two-minute boiled egg process.

How to Create a Process Map

1. Organize a team of subject matter experts (three to five members).
2. Educate them on principles and tools of process mapping.
3. Ask each to prepare a list of all related tasks for the defined process. It does not need to be in any order, just a list of all of the tasks performed in the process.
4. Schedule a two- to three-hour meeting to review compiled and enumerated tasks.
5. Create a list of agreed-on tasks.
   - Eliminate duplicate tasks.

- Evaluate all tasks by categorizing each task as "need to/must do," "like to do," and "nice to do."
6. Starting with a "start" block, place each task in order going top to bottom in the basic order in which the tasks are performed. When all of the tasks within a process are documented, end the map with an "end" block.
7. Hand off the list to your management engineering (ME) expert. A well-seasoned ME will clarify the first draft of the current-state process map.
8. At a follow-up meeting, the team reviews and evaluates the process map.

The map will look like Figure A.1. To ensure accuracy of the process map, all activities need to be sequenced and documented from top to bottom and from left to right. Figures A.2 and A.3 provide examples of completed process maps.

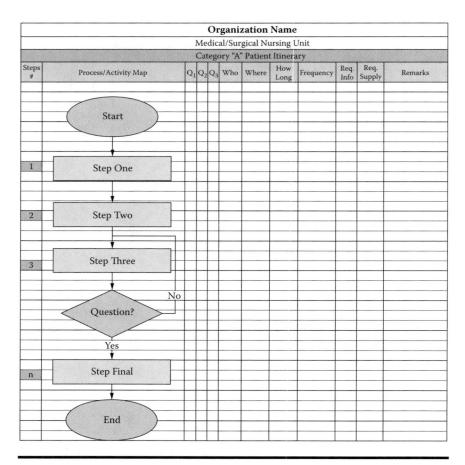

Figure A.1   Current-state map template.

ED Door to Doc Current State Process Map

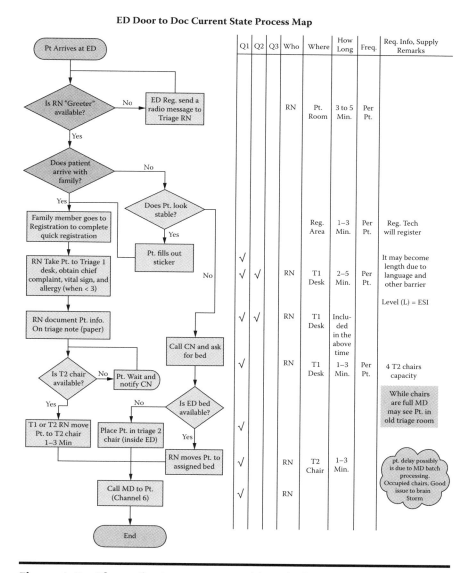

Figure A.2   The patient-care-centered hospital. CN = critical nursing; ED = emergency department; ESI = Emergency Services Level I; Pt = patient; Reg Tech = registration technician.

ED Door to Doc *Stabilized* "Future State" Process Map

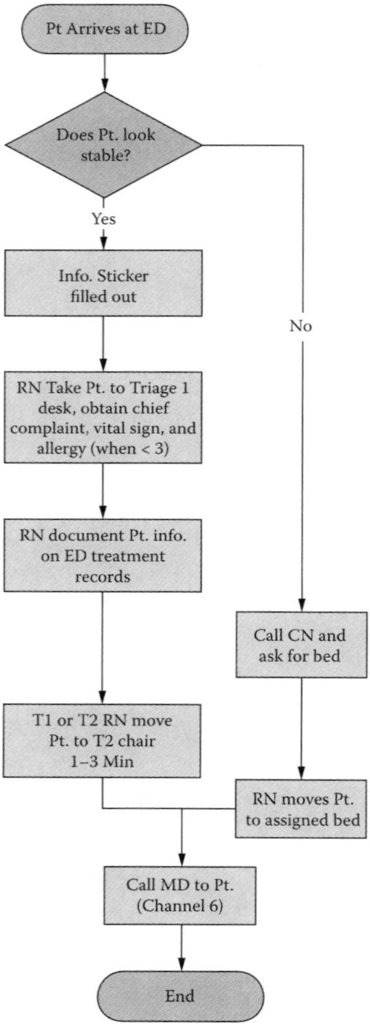

| | | | | | How | | Req. Info, |
Q1	Q2	Q3	Who	Where	Long	Frequency	Supply Remarks
√							
√	√		RN	T1 Desk	2–5 Min.	Per Pt.	It may become lengthy due to language and other barriers
√	√		RN	T1 Desk	Included in the above time	Per Pt.	
√							
√			RN	T1 Desk	1–3 Min.	Per Pt.	4 T2 chairs capacity
√			RN	T2 Chair	1–3 Min.	Per Pt.	
√							

Figure A.3   Example of a stabilized current-state map.

Appendix B: Process Description

Process Description		
Process Trait	**Vital Information**	**Explanation**
Process:	(Example: Final Patient Prep)	Task or activity name in Process Map
Map:	(Example: CCU Care Process – Day of Surgery)	Name of the Process Map
Step:	(Example: 3.4)	Step on Process Map
Created by:	(Example: Barb Smith, RN and Nick Wilson, P.E.)	Team who created the process description
Date update:	Example: YYYY/MM/DD)	Date of most recent update
Process owner:	(Example: Mary Jones, RN/ Pre-Op)	Department and department manager where the process is done
Process description:	For example, in the process map you may have a three minute process called "Take vital signs of patient." The process description should be detailed and look like the following: 1. introduce yourself to the patient 2. ask the patient their name for verification 3. check the blood pressure and temperature apparatuses 4. take the blood pressure 5. chart 6. take temperature 7. chart 8. …	This is a written document that replaces the standard procedure manual. It must explain in great detail each small step in the process and the order it should be done in.
Performed by:	(Example: Pre-surgery Nurse)	The labor classification that performs this task)
Customer requirements:	(Example: 20 minutes before surgery, showing concern for the patient)	A list of the requirements that the recipient requires for acceptable service
Measures:	For example: the % of surgeries with vital signs charted before the anesthesiology consult (Example: SMART Metrics)	The measurements used to determine process accuracy, reliability, and timeliness
Average time:	(Example: 6 minutes per patient)	Time for
Materials needed:	(Example: Electronic chart, blood pressure cuff, digital thermometer)	A list of materials needed to complete the process
Next step in the process:	(Example: Anesthesiologist/Patient Consult)	

Figure B.1   Process description template.

Appendix C: Example Project Starting with Functional Tree Structure

This appendix provides an example of the functional tree structure (FTS) process for a medical/surgical nursing department.

1. Organize a team of subject matter experts that includes the department director members (three to six individuals) and designate a facilitator. Provide two hours of training to help them with an introduction to operations improvement (OI), FTS, selected quality management tools, and process mapping.

2. Have the team create an initial high-level FTS of their area. Add to the structure the revenue and full-time equivalent (FTE) employees assigned to each of the functions. In this example, the 3N Medical/Surgical Nursing Unit was identified as the nursing unit that brought in the most revenue (Figure C.1).

3. The team then identifies, using available data (the number of cases by diagnosis-related group [DRG] treated in the unit), the patient types that are most frequently cared for in the unit (Figure C.2).

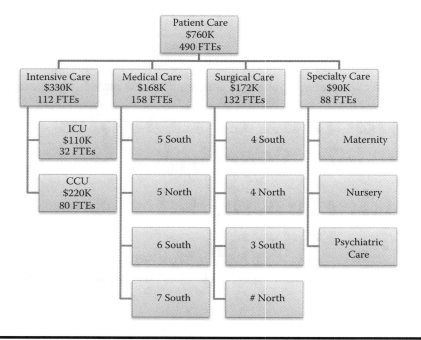

Figure C.1 **High level functional tree structure diagram.**

Medical Surgical Nursing Unit Patient Population			
MS DRG	MS DRG Description	Category	Number of Cases
470	Major joint replacement or reattachment of lower extremity w/o MCC		300
392	Esophagitis, gastroent & misc digest disorders w/o MCC		119
193	Simple pneumonia & pleurisy w MCC		75
189	Pulmonary edema & respiratory failure		66
641	Nutritional & misc metabolic disorders w/o MCC		64
690	Kidney & urinary tract infections w/o MCC		60
871	Septicemia w/o MV 96+ hours w MCC		54
603	Cellulitis w/o MCC		50

Figure C.2 **Prioritization matrix.**

4. Review the data (the number of cases by DRG) and determine whether the tasks associated with each DRG are similar to other DRGs. Using a team of process and clinical experts, group like DRGs based on disease etiology and treatment similarities. Similarities are defined by like

Medical Surgical Nursing Units		
Patient Volume by Categories		
DRG Categories	Sum of Number of Cases	Cumulative %
B	578	22.5%
A	485	41.5%
C and C, I	396	56.9%
D	178	63.8%
J	139	69.3%
E	131	74.4%
H	121	79.1%
I and I, C	105	83.2%
Other	431	100.0%

Figure C.3   Pareto chart showing DRG groups.

treatment schedule, supply utilization, labor (skill) utilization, and other characteristics (Figure C.3).

5. List the groups (the DRG categories in this example) in
descending order based on patient cases and create a
Pareto chart to identify the vital few and useful many processes within the unit as shown in Figure C.4.

6. For the 3N Medical/Surgical Nursing Unit, build a
detailed FTS diagram showing the DRG categories and
the primary task completed in servicing the patients who
fall into these categories. This task can also be done
by the subject matter experts and department director
(Figure C.5).

7. Starting with the task consuming the greatest amount of
resources, have the team members document all current
treatments, activities, and tasks performed for the targeted
processes. The form in Figure C.6 can be used. Allow
team members 48 hours to complete this homework.

8. The team's facilitator will compile all tasks and delete
duplicate tasks.

9. The team will then place the tasks in order regarding how
they are performed for each process. It is easier if the
team groups the services and activities done in the first

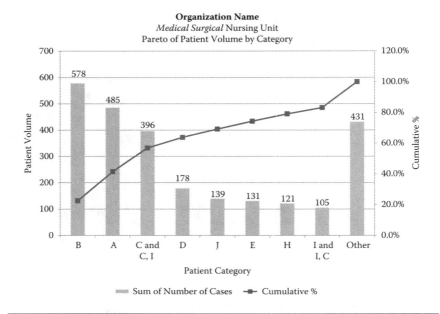

Figure C.4   Pareto chart showing DRG case volumes.

hour the patient is in the unit and then the second hour and so on until the discharge or transfer of the patient from the unit.

10. The team then evaluates each task as it relates to customer-defined criteria. In this process, the facilitator will attempt to include customer and expert feedback on the list. Any decisions or split in the process should be identified and the path between tasks drawn. With input from the experts and based on customer-defined criteria, the list can be simplified. At this time, the team should assemble a rough process map of the current operations.

11. The next step is to provide the simplified process map to a management engineer (ME; your process expert), who will create a current-state process map based on the information provided using the template in Figure C.7.

12. Reconvene the experts to validate each activity step of the process map developed by your ME. Review each step,

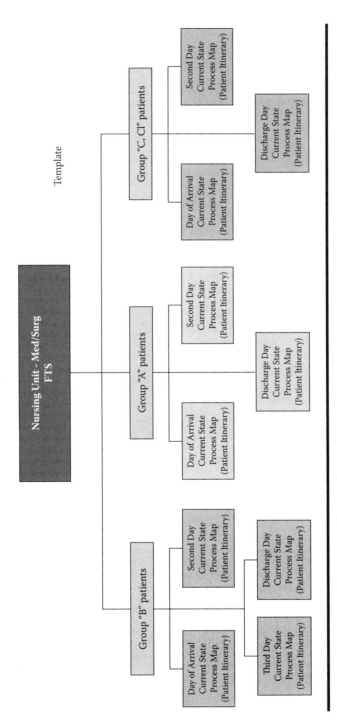

Figure C.5   Mid-level functional tree diagram.

				Hospital Name				
				Nursing Unit - Med/Surg				
				Patient Itinerary for (Category... "A")				
Rank	Day of the week	Hour of Patient Stay	SVCs #	Service and related activities Descriptions	Need to Do	Like to Do	Nice to Do
1	First Day	1st Hour	1	Admit Pt. to the unit			
2			2				
3		2nd Hour	1				
4		3rd Hour	1				
5			2				
6			3				
7							
8							
9							
10							
11							
12							
13							
14							
15							
16							
17							
18							
19							

Figure C.6   Listing of typical services provided.

asking the following questions, and extract any task that does not meet all three criteria:

- Does this step change the nature of the product/service?
- Is this step required by any credentialing or regulatory agency?
- Will the patient/customer be willing to pay for this step?

13. The team then completes the current-state process map by entering into the appropriate cells who performs the task, where the task is performed, how long it takes to complete on average, how often (frequency) the task is done, any required information needed to complete the task, and the required supply.

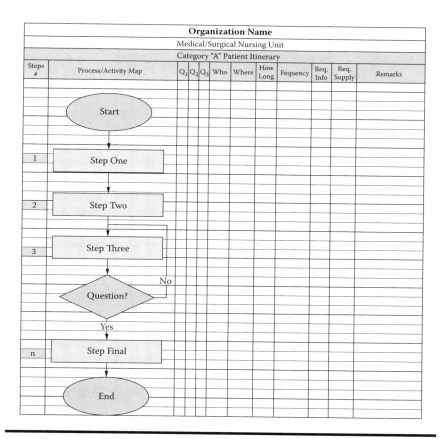

Figure C.7   Standard process map.

14. Complete the process description (Appendix B) and review with team members and nonteam members for accuracy.
15. Establish process output measures (SMART measures: simple, measurable, accurate and actionable, reliable and relevant, timely) that will convey process performance and patient/customer satisfaction.
16. Create staff training materials based on the process descriptions and the streamlined process map.
17. Initiate staff training; make sure that everyone is trained on the documented process map and process descriptions.

18. Implement the new process. Follow up with thorough training and monitoring until everyone follows the same processes.

Figure C.8 is an example of the first-day patient itinerary (current-state map) for the Medical/Surgical Nursing Unit.

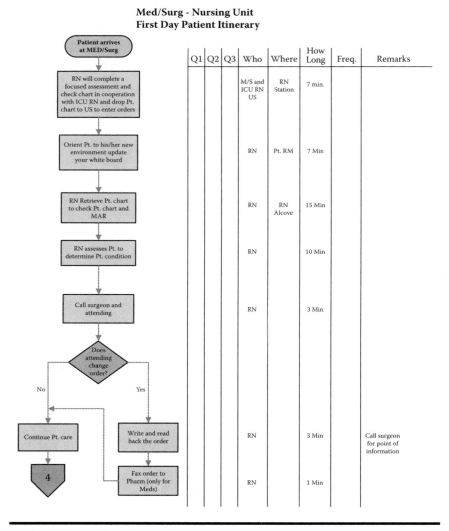

Figure C.8   Example current-state map.   *Continued*

Med/Surg - Nursing Unit First Day Patient Itinerary (Cont.)

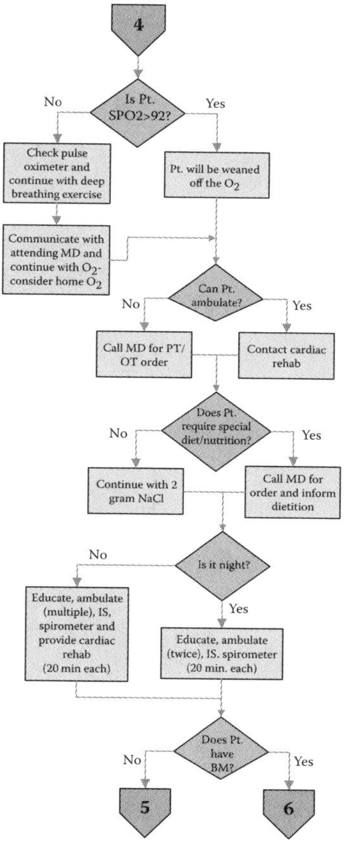

	Q1	Q2	Q3	Who	Where	How Long	Freq.	Remarks
				RN/CNA	Pt. Room	3 Min		
				RN	Pt. Room	3 Min		
				RN	Unit	3 Min		
				RN	Unit	20 Min		During day Cardiac Rehab will walk Pt. periodically

Figure C.8 (*Continued*) Example current-state map. *Continued*

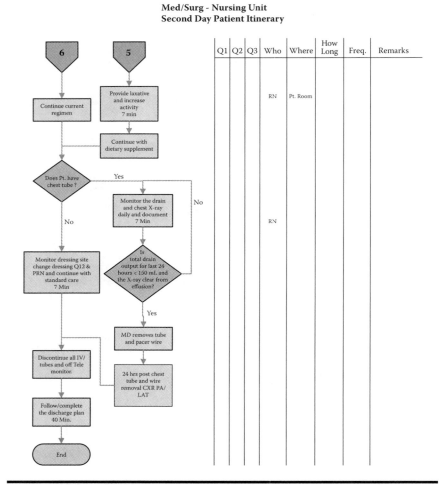

Figure C.8 (*Continued*)   Example current-state map.

Appendix D: Examples of Complete Functional Tree Structure

Functional Tree Structure Sampling

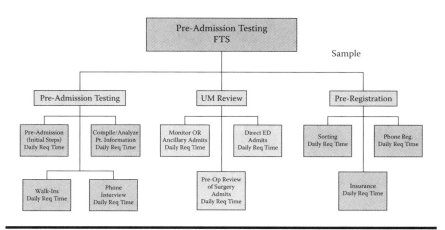

Figure D.1   High level functional tree structure diagram of the pre-admission testing function.

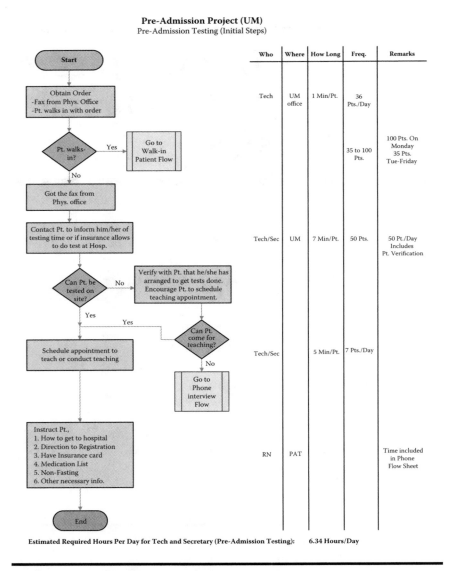

Figure D.2   Current-state process map for pre-admission testing.

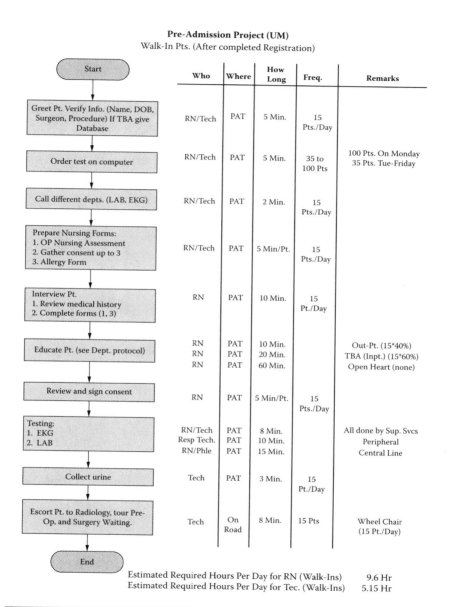

Figure D.3   Current-state process map for handling walk-in patients.

Pre-Admission Project (UM)
Phone Interview/Teaching

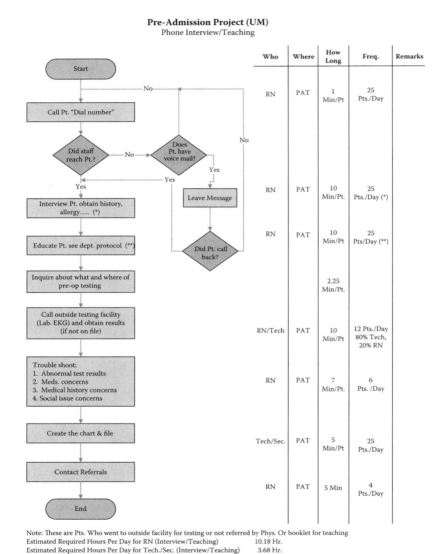

Note: These are Pts. Who went to outside facility for testing or not referred by Phys. Or booklet for teaching
Estimated Required Hours Per Day for RN (Interview/Teaching)   10.18 Hr.
Estimated Required Hours Per Day for Tech./Sec. (Interview/Teaching)   3.68 Hr.

Figure D.4 Current-state process map for conducting the pre-admission patient interview.

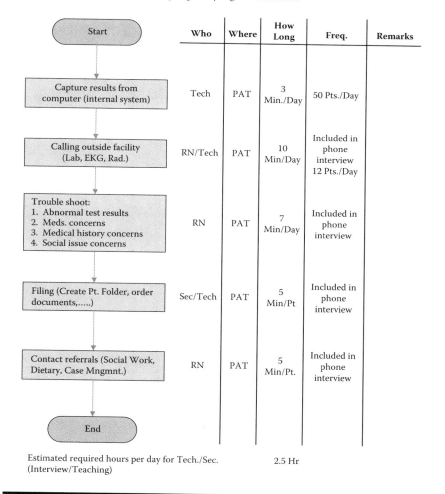

Figure D.5   Current-state process map for compiling pre-admission data.

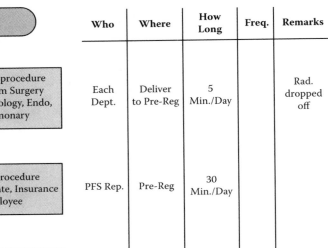

Pre-Admission Project (UM)
Compiling/Analyzing Pt. Information

Process	Who	Where	How Long	Freq.	Remarks
Start					
Obtain surgery/procedure notification from Surgery Scheduling, Radiology, Endo, Cardio-Pulmonary	Each Dept.	Deliver to Pre-Reg	5 Min./Day		Rad. dropped off
Sort surgery procedure notification by: Date, Insurance type, Employee	PFS Rep.	Pre-Reg	30 Min./Day		
Each employee receives his/her assigned portion of the notification	PFS Rep.	Pre-Reg	5 Min./Day		
Review for duplication	PFS Rep.	Pre-Reg	20 Min./Day		Total time for all reps.
End					

Total estimate required time/per day   60 Min.

Figure D.6   Current-state process map for reviewing surgical/procedure notification.

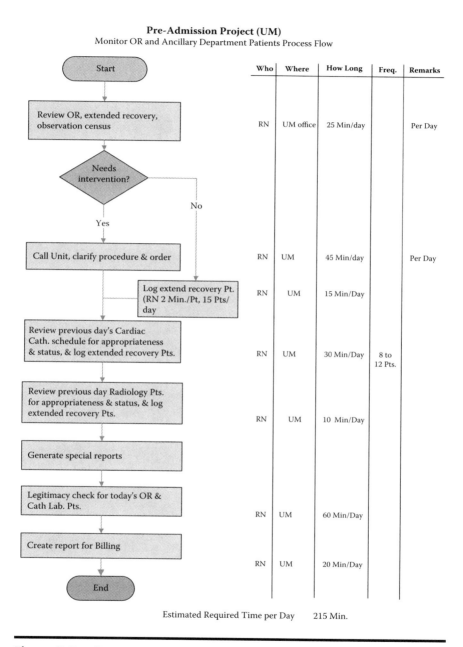

Pre-Admission Project (UM)
Monitor OR and Ancillary Department Patients Process Flow

Process	Who	Where	How Long	Freq.	Remarks
Review OR, extended recovery, observation census	RN	UM office	25 Min/day		Per Day
Call Unit, clarify procedure & order	RN	UM	45 Min/day		Per Day
Log extend recovery Pt. (RN 2 Min./Pt, 15 Pts/day	RN	UM	15 Min/Day		
Review previous day's Cardiac Cath. schedule for appropriateness & status, & log extended recovery Pts.	RN	UM	30 Min/Day	8 to 12 Pts.	
Review previous day Radiology Pts. for appropriateness & status, & log extended recovery Pts.	RN	UM	10 Min/Day		
Generate special reports					
Legitimacy check for today's OR & Cath Lab. Pts.	RN	UM	60 Min/Day		
Create report for Billing	RN	UM	20 Min/Day		

Estimated Required Time per Day   215 Min.

Figure D.7   Current-state process map for monitoring patient data.

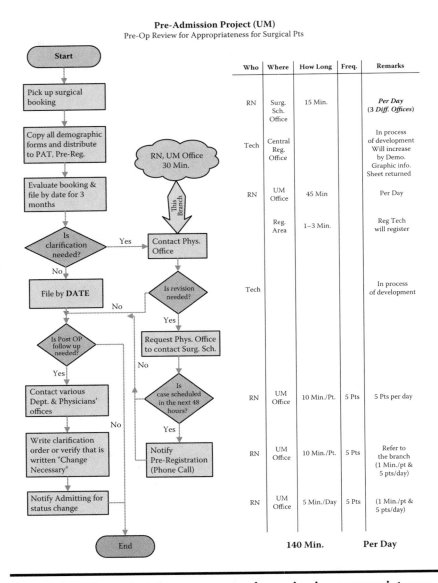

Figure D.8   Current-state process map for reviewing appropriateness for surgery.

Pre-Admission Project (UM)
Monitor ED and Direct Admit Process Flow

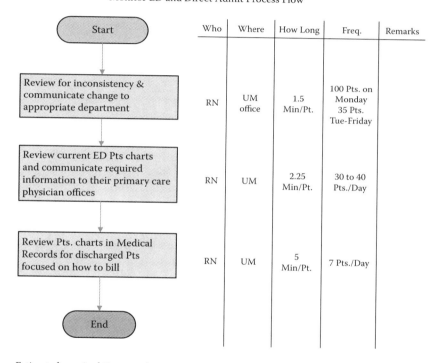

	Who	Where	How Long	Freq.	Remarks
Start					
Review for inconsistency & communicate change to appropriate department	RN	UM office	1.5 Min/Pt.	100 Pts. on Monday 35 Pts. Tue-Friday	
Review current ED Pts charts and communicate required information to their primary care physician offices	RN	UM	2.25 Min/Pt.	30 to 40 Pts./Day	
Review Pts. charts in Medical Records for discharged Pts focused on how to bill	RN	UM	5 Min/Pt.	7 Pts./Day	
End					

Estimated required time per day   186 Min.

Figure D.9   Current-state process map for emergency department and direct admit monitoring.

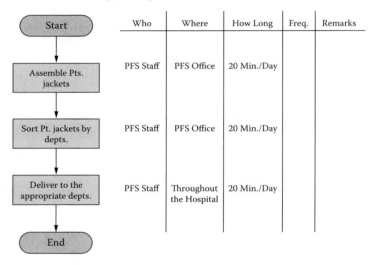

Total estimate required time/per day 60 Min.

Figure D.10 Current-state process map for sorting patient records.

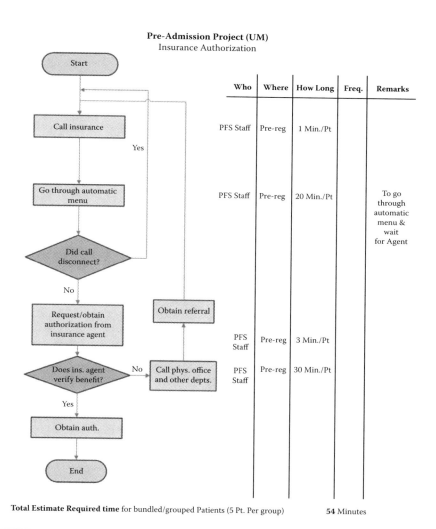

Pre-Admission Project (UM)
Insurance Authorization

	Who	Where	How Long	Freq.	Remarks
Call insurance	PFS Staff	Pre-reg	1 Min./Pt		
Go through automatic menu	PFS Staff	Pre-reg	20 Min./Pt		To go through automatic menu & wait for Agent
Request/obtain authorization from insurance agent	PFS Staff	Pre-reg	3 Min./Pt		
Call phys. office and other depts.	PFS Staff	Pre-reg	30 Min./Pt		

Total **Estimate Required time** for bundled/grouped Patients (5 Pt. Per group)   **54** Minutes

Figure D.11   Current-state process map for insurance authorization.

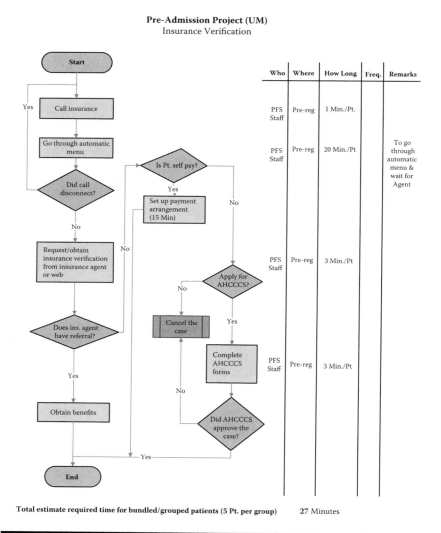

Figure D.12 Current-state process map for insurance verification.

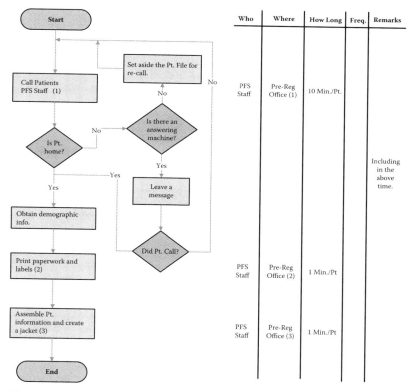

Pre-Admission Project (UM)
Phone Registration

Total estimate required time/per patient   12 Min.

Figure D.13   Current-state process map for phone registration.

Estimated Required FTE for Pre-Admission Redesign		
U M Review Req. Staffing		
Description	Hours	FTE Calc.
No. of Op. Days/Yr	255.7	
Total Minutes	138,341.4	
Required Hours	2,305.7	
20% of hrs assign to non-licensed staff	461.1	
Licensed Staff Hrs.	1,844.6	
Required FTE (Licensed Staff)		1.00
Req. FTE (Non-Licensed Staff)		0.25
Pre-Registration Req. Staffing		
Description	Hours	FTE Calc.
No. of Op. Days/Yr	255.7	
Daily Sorting Req. Hrs.	2.0	
Insurance		
Authorization	12.6	
Verification	6.3	
Phone Registration	10.0	
Total Hrs/Day	30.9	
Total Req. Hrs/Year	7,901.6	
Required FTE		4.27
Pre-Admission Testing Req. Staffing		
Description	Hours	FTE Calc.
No. of Op. Days/Yr	255.7	
Pre-Admission Initial Step		
Sec./Tech daily Req. Hrs.	6.4	
Walk-Ins		
RN daily Req. Hrs.	9.6	
Sec./Tech daily Req. Hrs.	5.2	
Phone Interview		
RN daily Req. Hrs.	10.2	
Sec./Tech daily Req. Hrs.	3.7	
Compile/Analyze Pt. Info.		
Sec./Tech daily Req. Hrs.	2.5	
Total RN Req Hrs/Year	5,058.0	
Total Sec./Tech. Req Hrs/Year	4,541.5	
Req. RN FTE.		2.73
Req. Sec./Tech FTE.		2.45
Total Req. RN		3.73
Req. Sec./Tech & Other		6.97

Figure D.14   Example full-time equivalent calculation.

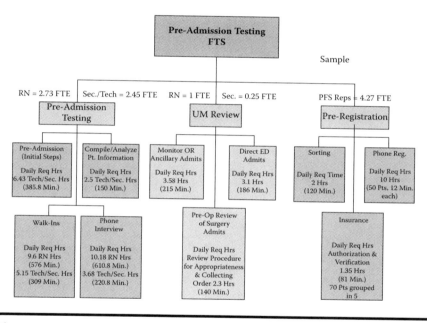

Figure D.15 **Final functional tree structure diagram of the pre-admission testing function.**

Index